...BE(AUSE you aRE **AWESOME** and a wonder-worker **YOU ARE GOD. JUST YOU.** PSALM 86:10

Celebrate Wonder All Ages is a curriculum that honors the spiritual life of children. *Celebrate Wonder All Ages* will engage children in open-ended exploration and inquiry of the Bible. Through experiential activities, spiritual practices, and reflection, *Celebrate Wonder All Ages* serves as a biblical guide to help children make meaning for their lives. This curriculum seeks to deepen children's faith formation and to create a safe space for children to ask big questions and claim their spiritual identity as children of God.

Please visit **CokesburyKids.com,** where you can find training videos, blog posts, free stuff, and more.

What Is...

Celebrate Wonder All Ages is a curriculum that seeks to celebrate spirituality through wonder. Children are naturally spiritual beings and everyday theologians. We want children to recognize and name this spirituality found within themselves and in all the world around them.

This curriculum is based on spiritual practices, which are incorporated through play, discovery, biblical exploration, faith conversation, and relationship. Children who participate in *Celebrate Wonder All Ages* will come to know and use spiritual practices as a way to deepen their faith and to grow in their spiritual identity as children of God. These spiritual practices then become building blocks for holy moments and enrich the faith lives of each and every child. We hope you will come wonder with us as we celebrate the Spirit of God in the lives of children.

The Components of...

Spiritual Practice

A spiritual practice is an intentional activity or ritual that helps you be aware of God's presence. For children, this means simple and tangible practices to connect to God's love.

Teaching children spiritual practices provides them with tools needed to fully know themselves as children of God. This is important because children who are equipped with these helpful daily practices can develop deeper connections to encounter the divine.

Children are innately spiritual. Their curiosity and wonder are a model for faith in action. Through spiritual practices, they can remain connected to this natural spirituality. Spiritual practices come in all shapes and sizes. In *Celebrate Wonder All Ages,* they are typically simple and interactive practices for the children to develop their own ways to feel God's presence and to know their identity as children of God.

Peaceful Place

The Peaceful Place is a space for the children to spend quiet time with God. Children enjoy having a comfortable place with quiet activities when they are feeling stressed or overwhelmed. Create a feeling of softness and rest by using soft rugs, pillows, and stuffed animals to snuggle with in the area. Each week there will be suggested books and quiet activities you can choose from. Since you know your children and what they need, you are invited to also include your own contributions to the Peaceful Place.

Wonder Table

A Wonder Table is similar to a worship altar found in many worship spaces. It is a holy space meant to help the children see and know God is present. We encourage you to use a smaller table that the children can see and interact with.

Each week there are suggested items to place on the table that coordinate with the church liturgical year and the Bible story. Suggested items include a Bible, a candle, a colored cloth, and so forth. The table can be used as a gathering area for the story time and for participating in spiritual practices.

Wonder Box

The Wonder Box is a special place to hold a special item that connects to the Faith Word and to the Bible story. Each week there will be a suggested item to place in the box. The Wonder Box is very special and is kept on the Wonder Table. Each week you will reveal what is inside and discuss its importance.

We encourage you to make your own Wonder Box. It can be any shape or size, but it's best if it has a lid. You can create your own box for the children, or you may wish to include the children in the creation process. The goal is for the children to come to know this box as very special. The Wonder Box is another way for the children to engage in the Bible story and to focus on the lesson.

Core Resources

C ELEBRATE W ONDER A LL A GES has been adapted to make it easy for ministry with children and families to happen, no matter what your church's current reality is. Whether you're meeting in-person all in one room, sending materials home for families to use together, offering a large group opening and small groups in-person or virtually, or hosting an intergenerational gathering for your whole church, C ELEBRATE W ONDER A LL A GES will work for you. The C ELEBRATE W ONDER A LL A GES Kit contains a Leader Guide, Reproducible Kids' Book, Class Pack, and CD-ROM! The CD-ROM has digital copies of the Leader Guide and Reproducible Kids' Book.

Kit:

Leader Guide

Reproducible Kids' Book

Class Pack

CD-ROM

Core Resources

Celebrate Wonder DVD

The *Celebrate Wonder DVD* features a child host who will engage the children through storytelling, life application, and exploration of the Faith Word. The DVD includes a music video and thirteen sessions (one for each Sunday) that are 3–5 minutes each.

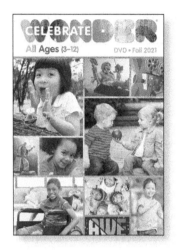

CEB Bible

This interactive Bible includes four-color icons and illustrations throughout, with a wealth of notes, historical facts, book introductions, devotionals, and other interactive elements to capture inquisitive young minds. The *Deep Blue Kids Bible* encourages a thirst for God's timeless message. For children ages 7–12.

Celebrate Wonder Bible Storybook

A colorfully illustrated children's Bible storybook that will engage the children through simple storytelling and open-ended questions that encourage the children to wonder about the Bible story and make connections between the Bible and their lives. Includes 150 stories!

Supplies

These are basic supplies you will want to have readily available. All supplies will be listed above the activity in the Leader Guide.

Box of tissues

Card stock

CD player

Chenille stems

Colored and white copy paper

Colored pencils

Computer and printer

Construction paper

Cotton balls

Cotton swabs

Crayons

DVD player

Glue, gluesticks

Hand-washing supplies

Index cards

Lunch-sized paper bags

Markers (washable and permanent)

Metal brads

Mural paper

Napkins

Paintbrushes

Paper bowls

Paper clips

Paper cups

Paper or plastic table coverings

Paper plates

Paper punch

Paper streamers

Paper towels

Pencils

Plastic containers for paint and water

Posterboard

Projector or television

Resealable plastic bags

Ribbon

Scissors (adult and safety)

Smocks

Stapler, staples

Stickers

Tape (clear, masking, and double-stick)

Tissue paper

Washable paint

Watercolor paints

Watercolor pencils

Wet wipes

Wooden craft sticks

Yarn

But forgiveness is with you—that's why you are honored. (Psalm 130:4)

Joseph and His Brothers – Genesis 37

Prepare to Wonder

Faith Word: RECONCILIATION

This unit we will focus on the spiritual practice of exploring reconciliation through forgiveness. The definition for reconciliation we will use is to bring peace between persons who have disagreed. The Bible is full of stories about disagreements and conflict, as well as forgiveness and reconciliation. Throughout Unit 1, we will talk about the conflict between Joseph and his brothers, and their final reconciliation.

The father of Joseph, Jacob, had twelve sons. Jacob considered Joseph the favorite of all his sons. He gave Joseph a special robe that we often refer to as "the robe of many colors." It was beautiful, and it had long sleeves. During Bible times, long-sleeved garments were for the privileged. Workers couldn't wear long sleeves because they would get in the way of their work. Joseph's brothers worked in the field with short-sleeved garments. Seeing Joseph with his long-sleeved robe filled the brothers with jealousy. They believed he was privileged since he did not have to work in the fields like they did.

The special robe was not the only reason the brothers resented Joseph. Joseph also had a gift for dreaming and interpreting dreams. He told his brothers of a dream where they bowed down to him. That was the last straw They decided to get rid of Joseph. The brothers decided to sell Joseph to a slave trader on his way to Egypt.

The brothers were jealous of Joseph, which led to conflict. Joseph may have added to the conflict by acting smug. There doesn't seem to be reconciliation in this Bible story. Reconciliation can take a long time. We have several more Bible stories about Joseph and his brothers. Look for signs leading to reconciliation as you read them.

Spiritual Practice for Adults

Joseph may have felt thankful his brothers didn't kill him, or he may have been mad at his brothers for selling him. Who has hurt you? Lie on your back and place your hand on your tummy. As you breathe in say, "I forgive (name of the person)." Breathe out and say, "I forgive (name the person)."

Come Together

Come Together

Supplies: Class Pack, Celebrate Wonder Bible Storybook, Wonder Box, robe with long sleeves, green cloth, battery-operated candle

Prepare Ahead: Set up a Wonder Table (see p. 3) with a green cloth, battery-operated candle, and a Wonder Box (see p. 3). Display the Unit 1 Bible Verse Poster (Class Pack—pp. 10 & 15) and Faith Word Poster (Class Pack—p. 4). Place the robe inside the Wonder Box.

- Point to the Unit 1 Faith Word Poster, and invite the children to wonder about what the word *reconciliation* means.

- Invite the kids to join you in a circle.

SAY: This month we will be hearing stories about a man named Joseph. Our story today is about Joseph and his twelve brothers.

ASK: Do you have any brothers? Do you have any sisters?

- In this curriculum, we recommend reading stories from the *Celebrate Wonder Bible Storybook*. Allow an elementary-age child to read the story, "Joseph and His Brothers" (pp. 42–43), from the storybook.

PRAY: Dear God, thank you for giving us families to love. Thank you that we can love our families. Amen.

"Joseph and His Brothers" Coloring Page – Preschool

Supplies: Reproducible Kids' Book, crayons

Prepare Ahead: Photocopy Reproducible 1A for each child.

- Invite the preschoolers to use crayons to color the picture. Share that Joseph had a special coat that was very colorful!

SAY: God thought Joseph was special. God thinks you are special!

Joseph's Coat – Younger Elementary

Supplies: Reproducible Kids' Book, crayons

Prepare: Photocopy "Joseph's Coat" (Reproducible 1B) for each child.

SAY: In today's Bible story, Jacob gave his son, Joseph, a robe to wear. Use the number code on the page to color Joseph's robe.

- Instruct the kids to use the number code to color in the spaces on Reproducible 1B. Provide assistance as needed. Preschoolers and older-elementary children may enjoy coloring the page as well.

Joseph's Brothers Word Search – Older Elementary

Supplies: *Reproducible Kids' Book, pencils or markers*

Prepare Ahead: *Photocopy "Joseph's Brothers Word Search" (Reproducible 1C) for each child.*

SAY: In today's Bible story, Jacob gave Joseph a special robe. Jacob's other sons were jealous. Joseph was Jacob's favorite son. Find the names of Joseph's brothers hidden in the word search. One brother's name is missing. Follow the directions at the bottom of the page to see which name is missing.

Stars and Snack – All Ages

Supplies: *Reproducible Kids' Book, hand-washing supplies, cereal with marshmallow shapes, medium-sized bowls, blue disposable plates, ladles or serving spoons*

Prepare Ahead: *Photocopy "September Stars and Constellations" (Reproducible 1D) for each kid in your class.*

- Invite the kids to wash their hands.
- Pour some cereal with marshmallow shapes into several medium bowls.
- Hand each kid a blue or dark blue disposable plate.
- Hand out a copy of Reproducible 1D to each child.
- Invite the kids to use the ladles or serving spoons to put one scoop of cereal on their plates.

SAY: In today's Bible story, Joseph has a special dream about the moon, the sun, and the stars of the night sky. Look at the star pictures on your sheet. Arrange the stars (or other marshmallow shapes) into star pictures like these.

- Help the kids as needed. When they are done "drawing" star pictures with the cereal, the kids may eat the cereal and marshmallows.

SAY: You can take your star sheet home and look for these stars in the sky!

Wonder Time

Interactive Bible Story

Supplies: *Reproducible Kids' Book*

Prepare Ahead: Photocopy today's Take-Home Pages from the Reproducible Kids' Book, 1F–1G (pp. 71–72). "Joseph and His Brothers" is written in short sections that are one to three sentences long. Invite several readers to take turns reading the story one section at a time. Display the Unit 1 Bible Verse Poster (Class Pack—pp. 10 & 15).

• Read through the story.

ASK: What do you think will happen to Joseph next?

Share a Story

Supplies: Celebrate Wonder DVD, TV, DVD player

• Invite the children to join you, sitting in a circle on the floor.

• Watch the Session 1 video (Celebrate Wonder DVD).

Wonder with Me

Supplies: Class Pack, Wonder Box, scissors

Prepare Ahead: Lay out the Unit 1 Wonder Story Mat (Class Pack—pp. 7 & 18). Cut out the five Unit 1 Bible story figures (Class Pack—p. 6).

• Place the Wonder Box on the Unit 1 Wonder Story Mat.

• Show the children the Unit 1 Faith Word Poster (Class Pack—p. 4).

SAY: *Reconciliation* is a big word! *Reconciliation* means to bring peace between persons who have disagreed.

• Point to the words on the Wonder Story Mat as you say them.

SAY: This word is *reconciliation,* which means to bring peace to people who disagree. This word is *forgiveness. Forgive* means to let go of any bad feelings about another person after that person has hurt you.

WONDER together:

❍ What does jealousy feel like?

• Place the figure of Joseph in his long robe and the figure of his five brothers on the Unit 1 Wonder Story Mat.

• Open the Wonder Box to reveal the robe.

WONDER: Why is a robe important in today's Bible story?

Experience Wonder

Joseph's "Bad Day" Game

Supplies: clean bathrobe, Hula-Hoop, office chair with wheels

Prepare Ahead: To set up the game, provide a clean bathrobe or similar garment. Next, place a Hula-Hoop in the room. Finally, provide an office chair with wheels.

- Today your class is learning about a very bad day for Joseph. To help the kids in your class learn what happened to Joseph, play this roleplay game.

SAY: In this game, you will pretend to be Joseph. Joseph had a very bad day!

- Choose one player to begin the game. Invite the player to put on the bathrobe. Then invite other kids in the class to (gently) remove the robe. This simulates Joseph's special robe being taken from him.

- Next, have the player jump into the Hula-Hoop and jump out. This simulates Joseph being thrown into a cistern.

- Last, have the player sit in the office chair. Invite one or two kids to slowly roll the chair to one end of the classroom. This simulates Joseph being taken away to Egypt.

- Have the player get out of the chair, and invite the others to roll the chair back where it had been.

- Play the game, allowing each kid who wants to participate to have a turn.

SAY: Joseph had a bad day. We'll learn more in our Bible story today.

Examine the Bible Verse

SAY: Our Unit 1 Bible verse is Psalm 130:4. Find it in your Bibles.

ASK: Is the Book of Psalms in the Old or New Testament? *(Old)* Where is Psalms located in the Old Testament? *(about the middle of your Bible)*

ASK: In what chapter is our verse located? *(130)* What is the verse number? *(4)*

- Gather the kids around the Unit 1 Bible Verse Poster. Read it together.

ASK: What is the reference for our verse? *(Psalm 130:4)*

SAY: Our Bible verse helps us understand that forgiveness comes from God. We will learn about forgiveness and reconciliation this month as we hear more about Joseph's story.

Peaceful Place

Supplies: Leader Guide—p. 113, Celebrate Wonder Bible Storybook, suggested book: "We All Need Forgiveness" by Mercer Mayer, fabric scraps, glue, paper, crayons

Prepare Ahead: Photocopy the Unit 1 Faith Word coloring sheet (Leader Guide—p. 113) for each child. Make extra copies of the Unit 1 Faith Word coloring sheet to leave in the Peaceful Place this month.

- Assist the children, as needed, as they interact with the items provided.

- Show the children how to glue fabric scraps onto paper.

- Give each child a piece of paper and have each child draw his or her favorite part of the story.

- Have each child color the Faith Word coloring sheet.

Tip: All of the supplies/activities suggested for the Peaceful Place are optional.

Go in Peace

Spiritual Practice – Exploring Reconciliation Through Forgiveness

Supplies: Leader Guide—pp. 111, 112

Prepare Ahead: Photocopy the "Celebration Chart" (p. 111) and the "Family Letter" (p. 112). Make a copy of both for each child.

SAY: A spiritual practice is something we do to help us connect to God. This week we talked about the conflict between Joseph and his brothers. We also talked about forgiveness. *Forgiveness* means to let go of any bad feelings about another person after that person has hurt you.

- Guide the children through a spiritual practice.

SAY: Lie down and place your hands on your tummy.

SAY: Say, "I'm mad," as you exhale and watch your tummy get small. Say, "I forgive," as you exhale and watch your tummy grow with God's love.

PRAY: Repeat after me: "God, help me to forgive myself and others. Amen."

- Bless the children before they leave. Touch each child as you say this blessing: "May you always carry forgiveness in your heart. God bless you."

Family Spiritual Practice

SAY: Let's take a look at your Take-Home Pages (Reproducibles 1F–1G). Ask your family to read the Bible story and participate in this week's spiritual practice with you. There's an extra activity for you to do sometime this week.

Supplemental Activities

Preschoolers – Retell the Story with Song

- Have the children interact with the Unit 1 Bible story figures (Class Pack—p. 6) as you sing the song.

- Sing these verses several times to the tune of "The Farmer in the Dell."

SING: Joseph had a robe. His brothers, they were mad. / Joseph had a robe. His brothers, they were mad. / The robe had many colors because of Joseph's special robe. / Joseph had a robe. His brothers, they were mad.

SAY: We know that Joseph's brothers were mad that Joseph had a dream that his brothers bowed down to him. That made them very angry!

WONDER: What do you think a dream showing the brothers bowing down to Joseph might mean? Why would that dream make his brothers mad?

Early Elementary – Robe Relay

Supplies: one short robe and one long robe for each team, masking tape

Prepare Ahead: Use masking tape to create a start line and a finish line for each team. Place a short robe at the start line for each team and a long robe or tunic at the finish line for each team.

SAY: In the Bible story, Jacob gave Joseph a special robe. Usually, men would wear short robes with short sleeves so they could easily get their work done. Only women would wear long robes with long sleeves. When Jacob gave Joseph a long robe, his brothers were not only jealous because it was beautiful but because the long robe meant that Joseph would not be expected to work. Do you think it would be harder to work in a long robe than a short robe?

SAY: Let's have a relay race.

- Split the children into teams, and have each team line up behind the start line you create. Give these directions:

  ○ Put on the short robe at the starting line.

  ○ Walk/jog to the finish line.

  ○ Take off the short robe and leave it there. Put on the long robe.

  ○ Walk/jog to the start line and take of the long robe.

  ○ Tag the next child to start his or her turn in the relay by putting on the long robe.

- Make sure the children are lined up in their places. Then count back from five and say, "Go." The first team to finish the relay with every team member wins.

Older Elementary – Magnet Science

Supplies: magnets

Prepare Ahead: Be sure to try your magnets ahead of time to make sure they work to display the message you are hoping for.

WONDER: What does it feel like to be in conflict with someone else?

- Use the magnets to show how conflict can turn us apart and reconciliation or forgiveness can bring us back together in relationship again by holding the magnets up, showing opposing ends that push against each other.

SAY: This might be an example of us and others in conflict. Notice the two magnets push each other away. *(Use the magnets to demonstrate.)* Now, if one is willing to turn from conflict and offer reconciliation, then you will see that both people are now drawn together. *(This should also work if both begin to turn.)*

ASK: What surprised you about what you saw the magnets do? What does this activity tell you about reconciliation? Have you ever resolved a conflict and felt closer to the other person than before?

- Let the children discuss, as time permits.

Intergenerational Activity – Shirt of Many Colors

Note: Each week we will feature a special intergenerational activity. Plan to invite youth and adults to join you for these special activities.

Supplies: See Reproducible 1E.

Prepare Ahead: Photocopy Reproducible 1E to give to each group.

- This week make tie-dye shirts together! Invite all participants to wear old clothes or provide smocks for them to wear. Provide the materials outlined on "Shirt of Many Colors" (Reproducible 1E). Make sure to pre-wash the T-shirts.

- Invite other adults to help you set up the activity in an outdoor area or other place where making a mess is allowed.

- Group the kids in your class with youth and adults. Make sure each group has a good mix of young and old from your church.

SAY: Joseph was given a colorful or highly decorated coat to wear. Use the directions on your sheet to make colorful tie-dye shirts!

- Invite the groups to make their tie-dye shirts. Shirts should be given time to air-dry before taking them home.

But forgiveness is with you—that's why you are honored. (Psalm 130:4)

Joseph in Egypt – Genesis 39:20–40:23

Prepare to Wonder

Faith Word: RECONCILIATION

Reconciliation is a big word for little ones. Reconciliation can be hard to understand for adults, as well as children. Forgiving someone does not necessarily bring about reconciliation. Reconciliation restores a right relationship with the person you are in conflict with. Reconciliation can be a slow process, not unlike growing a plant. The seed must be planted in good soil. It must be nurtured and cared for as it grows. The seed of reconciliation must be planted in a truly remorseful person, who takes the time to nurture and care for the person wronged. Eventually, as a seed may bloom, a relationship may be restored.

The Bible story this week tells us about the dreams Joseph had. Joseph believed the dreams came from God. Joseph also believed his ability to interpret the dreams came from God. In the Bible story this week, Joseph was in prison for something he did not do. Instead of complaining and losing hope, Joseph used his gift of dream interpretation for the pharaoh's baker and cupbearer. Joseph correctly interpreted the events that would unfold and that will help him in next week's lesson.

Joseph was treated badly, and that would have made many people angry and mad. Not Joseph. He continued to use the opportunities God provided him to grow seeds of reconciliation. Joseph continues to mature and learn from each unfortunate event.

Spiritual Practice for Adults

Imagine you are frustrated and angry with God. You don't like being angry with God; you feel terrible inside. You know you shouldn't feel this way, but you do. What would you do? Pray? Some of the steps in reconciliation are the same we take when we pray. Confess your anger with God and your part in it. Say you are sorry for feeling the way you do. Commit to changing your behavior, and pray God will grant you peace.

Come Together

Come Together

Supplies: Class Pack, Celebrate Wonder Bible Storybook, Wonder Box, green cloth, battery-operated candle, small pillow

Prepare Ahead: Set up a Wonder Table (see p. 3) with a green cloth, battery-operated candle, and a Wonder Box (see p. 3). Display the Unit 1 Bible Verse Poster (Class Pack—pp. 10 & 15) and Faith Word Poster (Class Pack—p. 4). Place a small pillow inside the Wonder Box.

- Point to the Unit 1 Faith Word Poster, and invite the children to wonder about what the word *reconciliation* means.

- Invite the kids to join you in a circle.

SAY: This month we are hearing stories about a man named Joseph. Our story today is about what happened to Joseph in the land of Egypt.

ASK: Do you remember what happened to Joseph in last week's story?

- Take a few minutes to talk about last week's Bible story.

- We recommend reading a story each week from the *Celebrate Wonder Bible Storybook*. Allow an elementary kid to read, "Joseph in Egypt" (pp. 44–45), from the storybook.

PRAY: Dear God, Joseph helped others. Guide us to help others too. Amen.

Prisoner's Dream – Preschool

Supplies: Reproducible Kids' Book, crayons

Prepare Ahead: Photocopy "A Prisoner's Dream (1)" (Reproducible 2A) and "A Prisoner's Dream (2)" (Reproducible 2B) for each preschooler.

- Invite the preschoolers to use crayons to color the picture. Invite elementary kids to help the preschoolers follow the directions on the pages.

SAY: God thought Joseph was special. God thinks you are special!

Prisoner's Dream – Younger Elementary

Supplies: Reproducible Kids' Book, crayons, colored pencils

Prepare Ahead: This week Reproducibles 2A and 2B can be shared with all of the kids in your class. You may have already shared them with your preschoolers. Photocopy Reproducibles 2A and 2B for all the kids in your class.

- Have crayons and colored pencils available, and invite the class to color the pages using the directions at the top.

Silly Story – Older Elementary

Supplies: *Reproducible Kids' Book, pencils*

Prepare Ahead: *Photocopy "Silly Story" (Reproducible 2C) for each child.*

SAY: Fill in the blanks using silly words. Then find Genesis 39–40 in a *Common English Bible* to learn the correct answers.

- Invite the kids to fill the blanks according to the word prompts indicated on the page under each blank line.
- Assist the kids if they get stuck or suggest they work together if needed.
- Then have the kids use Bibles to find the story. Invite them to compare their silly stories to the story from the Bible.

Bagels and Juice – All Ages

Supplies: *paper cups, juice, napkins, nitrile gloves, bagels, cream cheese or butter, paper plates, plastic knives or clean craft sticks, optional: toaster*

SAY: In today's Bible story, two prisoners have dreams. One prisoner had been the pharaoh's cupbearer.

- Hold up a disposable cup and pour some juice in it.

SAY: The other prisoner had been the pharaoh's baker.

- Wearing a nitrile glove, hold up a bagel.

SAY: Let's enjoy a breakfast treat this morning as we think about our Bible story from last week.

- Invite the kids to enjoy a plain or toasted bagel with cream cheese or butter. Older-elementary kids will enjoy helping younger kids with their breakfast snack.
- Pour cups of fruit juice for the kids to enjoy with their bagels.
- As the kids eat, talk about last week's Bible story ("Joseph and His Brothers").
- Invite the kids to help clean up after the snack.

Wonder Time

Interactive Bible Story

Supplies: *Reproducible Kids' Book*

Prepare Ahead: Photocopy today's Take-Home Pages from the Reproducible Kids' Book, 2F–2G (pp. 73–74). "Joseph in Egypt" is written in short sections that are one to three sentences long. Display the Unit 1 Bible Verse Poster (Class Pack—pp. 10 & 15).

- Invite several readers to take turns reading the story, one section at a time.

ASK: What do you think will happen to Joseph next?

Share a Story

Supplies: Celebrate Wonder DVD, TV, DVD player

- Invite the children to join you, sitting in a circle on the floor.
- Watch the Session 2 video (Celebrate Wonder DVD).

Wonder with Me

Supplies: Class Pack, Wonder Box, scissors

Prepare Ahead: Lay out the Unit 1 Wonder Story Mat (Class Pack—pp. 7 & 18). Cut out the three remaining Unit 1 story figures (Class Pack—6), if not done already.

- Place the Wonder Box on the Unit 1 Wonder Story Mat.

SAY: Today's Faith Word is *reconciliation*.

- Show the children the Unit 1 Faith Word Poster (Class Pack—p. 4).

SAY: Last week we talked about *reconciliation*, a big word meaning to bring peace between persons who have disagreed.

- Point to the words on the Unit 1 Wonder Story Mat.

SAY: This word is *reconciliation,* which means to bring peace to people who disagree. This word is *forgiveness.* You forgive so you can be reconciled and stay friends with those you disagree with. Joseph had a special gift of interpreting dreams.

WONDER together:

- ❍ Do you have a special gift?
- ❍ How can you use your special gift to bring peace?
- ❍ Which of these words describes our Bible story: *reconciliation* or *forgiveness*?

- Add the figure of Joseph in his white tunic on the Wonder Story Mat.
- Open the Wonder Box to reveal the pillow.

WONDER: I wonder why a pillow is in the Wonder Box.

Experience Wonder

Sleep Tag

SAY: When we are awake, we are always busy. We only dream when we are asleep. Sleeping gives us time to dream. Joseph had special dreams when he slept. His dreams often told him what could happen in the future. Sleeping and resting are important. Let's practice resting with a game.

- When the lights are on, have the children busily run around the room. When the lights are off, have them lie on the floor and close their eyes.

- Play several rounds, leaving the light off longer each time.

WONDER: Do you remember any special dreams you have had? What was important about your dream(s)? What do you think is important about the Bible story?

Examine the Bible Verse

SAY: Our Unit 1 Bible verse is Psalm 130:4. Find it in your Bibles.

ASK: Is the Book of Psalms in the Old or New Testament? *(Old)* Where is Psalms located in the Old Testament? *(about the middle of your Bible)* In what chapter of Psalms is our verse located? *(130)* What is the verse number? *(4)*

- Gather the kids around the Unit 1 Bible Verse Poster. Read it together.

ASK: What is the reference for our verse? *(Psalm 130:4)*

SAY: Our Bible verse helps us understand that forgiveness comes from God. We will learn about forgiveness and reconciliation as we hear more about Joseph's story.

Roller Coaster Ride

Supplies: Reproducible Kids' Book, foam pipe insulation, rolls of masking tape, marbles

Prepare Ahead: Get a few pieces of foam pipe insulation from your local hardware store or home improvement store. You will be dividing your class into teams of two to three kids. So, make sure you have a piece of insulation for each group. Photocopy "Roller Coaster Ride" (Reproducible 2D) for each group.

- Divide your class into groups of two to three kids. Hand each group a roll of masking tape.

- Hand out copies of Reproducible 2D to each group.

SAY: Joseph's life had a lot of ups and downs—kind of like a roller coaster!

ASK: Have any of you ridden a roller coaster?

• Invite the kids to share their roller coaster experiences.

SAY: Some roller coasters have a big loop in the track. When you ride them, you go upside down as the coaster zooms through the loop! In this activity, use the picture on your sheet to make a loop. Try placing a marble on your "roller coaster" and see if it will zoom through the loop!

• Instruct the groups to attach one end of their insulation to a wall, table, or chair. By taping the insulation into place along the wall, table, chair, and floor, they can create a loop that will actually make the marble go upside down, but stay on the "track"!

• This activity will work, but it takes some experimentation. Allow the groups to try a few times, but offer help if they get stuck. For a hint, a small loop at the end of the insulation (taped to the floor) works best.

SAY: In this activity, we see that the force of the marble going through the loop is stronger than the force that would normally make the marble drop to the ground. Joseph was able to manage his ups and downs because God was a powerful force in his life.

Peaceful Place

Supplies: Reproducibles 2A–2B (Reproducible Kids' Book), Unit 1 Bible story figures (Class Pack—p. 6), Celebrate Wonder Bible Storybook, suggested book: "Harriet, You'll Drive Me Wild!" by Mem Fox, sand tray, soft pillows, crayons or markers

• Assist the children, as needed, as they interact with the items provided.

• Have the children use their fingers in the sand tray as they imagine walking to Egypt.

Tip: All of the supplies/activities suggested for the Peaceful Place are optional.

Go in Peace

Spiritual Practice – Exploring Reconciliation Through Forgiveness

SAY: A spiritual practice is something we do to help us connect to God. God wants us to forgive others. Forgiving and reconciling with others helps us grow closer. We practiced saying we were sorry earlier.

- Guide the children through a spiritual practice:
  - ○ Think of someone you have hurt and you need to say you are sorry to. Imagine saying sorry to them. Imagine they say you are forgiven.

PRAY: Repeat after me: "God, thank you for helping me forgive those who hurt me. Amen."

SAY: This week remember to ask for forgiveness and forgive those who hurt you.

- Bless the children before they leave. Touch each child as you say this blessing: "May you always carry forgiveness in your heart. God bless you."

Family Spiritual Practice

SAY: Let's take a look at your Take-Home Pages for today (*Reproducibles 2F–2G*). Ask your family to participate in this week's spiritual practice.

Supplemental Activities

Preschoolers – Retell the Story with Song

- Have the children interact with the Unit 1 Bible story figures (Class Pack—p. 6) as you sing the song.
- Sing the verses to the tune of "The Farmer in the Dell."

SING: To Egypt, Joseph went. / To Egypt, Joseph went. / The Lord was with young Joseph. / To Egypt, Joseph went.

SAY: Last week Joseph was given a special robe from his father, Jacob. The robe made Joseph's brothers mad, so they sold him to a man who took him to Egypt.

ASK: What happened to Joseph in the Bible story today?

WONDER: Which part of the story did you like? Which part did you not like?

Early Elementary – Dream Art

Supplies: paper, crayons or markers

WONDER: The baker and the cupbearer had dreams. What do you dream about? Do you ever remember your dreams?

- Give each child a some paper and something to draw with.
- Invite each child to each draw a dream he or she had or of one of the prisoners' dreams.

Older Elementary – God's Dream

Supplies: black construction paper, chalk or chalk pastels

SAY: In the Bible story, Joseph helped Pharaoh's workers interpret their dreams. Dreams can be amazing and interesting things! Do you remember your dreams? What do you think God's dreams for our world are? Do you think God's dream includes reconciliation? If so, what might reconciliation look like?

- Give each child a black piece of construction paper and chalk or chalk pastels.

- Instruct the children to reflect on the questions and conversation from above.

- Invite the children to answer the question: What are God's dreams for our world? Perhaps you might write that on a poster or board where they can see it.

- Invite wonder and imagination as they create.

- When they are done creating, make sure to leave time for the group to share and discuss. Point out themes of God's reconciliation, love, and care for us.

Intergenerational Activity – Food Collection

Note: Each week we will feature a special intergenerational activity. Plan to invite youth and adults to join you for these activities.

Supplies: Reproducible Kids' Book

Prepare Ahead: Photocopy "Food Donation Items" (Reproducible 2E) and hand copies out to your class and to other members of the church.

- This week plan a food drive for your church.

- Plan how the food drive will work. For example, you might invite church members to bring food donations to your church building for the next few weeks. Then decide if a food pantry or other group will receive your donations.

SAY: We will learn more about the food drive in Session 3.

But forgiveness is with you—that's why you are honored. (Psalm 130:4)

Joseph Saves the Day – Genesis 41:1-57

Prepare to Wonder

Faith Word: Reconciliation

When we left Joseph last week, he was still in prison. Joseph had correctly interpreted a dream for the pharaoh's cupbearer two years earlier. Joseph asked the cupbearer to remember him and tell the pharaoh about him when the cupbearer returned to work, but the cupbearer forgot.

The pharaoh began to have dreams he did not understand. He knew the dreams were important, but none of his advisors or religious leaders could tell him what the dreams meant. The cupbearer remembered Joseph and told the pharaoh how Joseph had correctly interpreted his dreams when he was in prison.

The pharaoh summoned Joseph from prison. Before Joseph heard the dreams, he told the pharaoh that God sent the dreams, and it was God who would provide the interpretation, not Joseph. Pharaoh's dreams included seven fat cows followed by seven skinny cows, and seven healthy stalks of grain followed by seven weak stalks of grain. Joseph informed Pharaoh his dreams meant God was going to send seven years of abundance followed by seven years of severe famine. He offered advice to the pharaoh and recommended a wise person be appointed to take charge of the grain harvest.

Pharaoh took his advice and appointed Joseph to be second-in-command to insure the people were taken care of in the years of famine. Joseph did not know events would soon take shape that would give him and his brothers a chance to reconcile.

Spiritual Practice for Adults

Have you had hurts you have been unable to get rid of? Grab a bottle of bubbles and think of a hurt you have and the person who gave it to you. As the bubbles float away, imagine your hurts floating away. Pray that God will help you forgive.

Come Together

Come Together

Supplies: Class Pack, Celebrate Wonder Bible Storybook, Wonder Box, green cloth, battery-operated candle, seven small toy cows

Prepare Ahead: Set up a Wonder Table (see p. 3) with a green cloth, battery-operated candle, and a Wonder Box (see p. 3). Display the Unit 1 Bible Verse Poster (Class Pack—pp. 10 & 15) and Faith Word Poster (Class Pack—p. 4). Place the seven cows inside the Wonder Box.

- Point to the Unit 1 Faith Word Poster, and invite the children to wonder about what the word *reconciliation* means.
- Invite the kids to join you in a circle.

SAY: Our story today is about how Joseph saved the day.

ASK: Do you remember what happened to Joseph in last week's story?

- Take a few minutes to talk about last week's Bible story.
- We recommend reading a story each week from the *Celebrate Wonder Bible Storybook.* Allow an elementary kid to read, "Joseph Saves the Day" (pp. 46–47), from the storybook.

PRAY: Dear God, Joseph helped others. Guide us to help others too. Amen.

Joseph Saves the Day – Preschool

Supplies: Reproducible Kids' Book, crayons, pencils

Prepare Ahead: Photocopy Reproducible 3A for each preschooler.

- Invite the preschoolers to use crayons to color the picture. Invite elementary kids to help the preschoolers follow the directions on the page.

SAY: God thought Joseph was special. God thinks you are special!

Pharaoh's Dream – Younger Elementary

Supplies: Reproducible Kids' Book, pencils

Prepare Ahead: Photocopy "Pharaoh's Dream" (Reproducible 3B) for each child.

SAY: Pharaoh had a confusing dream. Joseph helped Pharaoh "decode" the confusing dream. Use the code key at the bottom of this page to help Joseph.

- Allow the kids to work on the page. The kids may work together.

ASK: What message did you find?

SAY: Pharaoh had strange dreams. In his dreams, he saw seven fat cows. Then he saw seven thin cows. These dreams had an important meaning. We'll learn more about what the dreams meant in today's session.

The Dream Team – Older Elementary

Supplies: Reproducible Kids' Book, pencils, crayons or markers

Prepare Ahead: Photocopy "The Dream Team" (Reproducible 3C) for each child.

SAY: In today's Bible story, Joseph became the second-in-command in Egypt! Design a poster promoting Pharaoh and Joseph as "The Dream Team."

- Allow the kids to work on their posters.
- After the kids have had time to work, invite them to share their posters.

Egyptian Hieroglyphs – All Ages

Supplies: Reproducible Kids' Book, paper, card stock, crayons, colored pencils, markers, scissors, banner paper and way to hang it on classroom walls, posterboard

Prepare Ahead: Photocopy "Egyptian Hieroglyphs" (Reproducible 3D) for each kid in your class. Gather supplies. You do not necessarily need to include all these supplies. This will be an open art activity where the kids can decide what kind of art they wish to make.

SAY: Ancient Egyptians used a kind of writing called *hieroglyphs*. Hieroglyphs use word pictures as a large alphabet for writing things down. Use the hieroglyphs on the page to make your own piece of art.

- Make the art materials available to the class.
- Invite the kids to make a hieroglyph piece of art on paper or card stock. You may also invite a group of kids to hang a large sheet of banner paper on the wall.
- Allow the kids to work on their art.

SAY: In ancient Egypt, these pictures were a way of writing down ideas.

ASK: What do you think the different word pictures mean?

- Invite the kids to make guesses about what the word pictures might mean.
- Encourage the kids to take their hieroglyph art and reference sheets with them today and make more projects at home.

Wonder Time

Interactive Bible Story

Supplies: Reproducible Kids' Book

Prepare Ahead: Photocopy today's Take-Home Pages from the Reproducible Kids' Book, 3F–3G (pp. 75–76). "Joseph Saves the Day" is written in short sections that are one to three sentences long. Invite several readers to take turns reading the story one section at a time. Display the Unit 1 Bible Verse Poster (Class Pack—pp. 10 & 15).

• Read through the story.

ASK: What do you think will happen to Joseph next?

Share a Story

Supplies: Celebrate Wonder DVD, TV, DVD player

• Invite the children to join you, sitting in a circle on the floor.

• Watch the Session 3 video (Celebrate Wonder DVD).

Wonder with Me

Supplies: Class Pack, Wonder Box, scissors

Prepare Ahead: Lay out the Unit 1 Wonder Story Mat (Class Pack—pp. 7 & 18). Cut out the two remaining Unit 1 story figures (Class Pack—p. 6), if not already done.

• Place the Wonder Box on the Unit 1 Wonder Story Mat.

SAY: In this unit, we are using this definition for *reconciliation:* to bring peace between persons who have disagreed.

• Point to the words on the Unit 1 Wonder Story Mat.

SAY: This word is *reconciliation,* which means to bring peace to people who disagree. This word is *forgiveness. Forgive* means to let go of any bad feelings about another.

WONDER together:

❍ How did Joseph's interpretation of the pharaoh's dream help the pharaoh and Egypt?

❍ Why did Joseph tell the pharaoh his gift of interpreting dreams came from God?

❍ Which of these words would you use to describe today's Bible story?

- Place the Bible story figure of Pharaoh on the Wonder Story Mat.
- Open the Wonder Box to reveal the seven cows.

WONDER: Why are there seven cows in the Wonder Box?

Experience Wonder

Fat Cows, Thin Cows

SAY: Pharaoh had strange dreams. In his dreams, he saw seven fat cows. Then he saw seven thin cows.

- Invite the kids to sit on the floor.
- Demonstrate how to act like a fat cow. Have the kids puff their cheeks up with air.
- Next, demonstrate how to act like a thin cow. Have the kids suck in their cheeks.
- Invite the class to close their eyes. When you say, "Go," the kids should act like fat cows or thin cows. Instruct them to stay that way until you say, "Open."
- As they open their eyes and look around the room, have them continue to stay "fat" or "thin" as you count. Did you have more fat cows or thin cows?
- Continue playing the game as time allows.

SAY: Pharaoh's dreams had a meaning. We will learn more about what his dreams meant in today's session.

Examine the Bible Verse

SAY: Our Unit 1 Bible verse is Psalm 130:4. Find it in your Bibles.

ASK: Is the Book of Psalms in the Old or New Testament? *(Old)* Where is Psalms located in the Old Testament? *(about the middle of your Bible)* In what chapter of Psalms is our verse located? *(130)* What is the verse number? *(4)*

- Gather the kids around the Unit 1 Bible Verse Poster. Read it together.

ASK: What is the reference for our verse? *(Psalm 130:4)*

SAY: Our Bible verse helps us understand that forgiveness comes from God. We will learn about forgiveness and reconciliation as we hear more about Joseph's story.

Bible Verse Puzzle Pieces

Supplies: Reproducible Kids' Book, white or colored card stock, laminator and laminating supplies, one or more shallow containers, play sand or small pebbles, scissors

Prepare Ahead: Photocopy one or more copies of "Bible Verse Puzzle Pieces" (Reproducible 3E) onto white or colored card stock. You may choose to make one or more sets of the puzzle pieces depending on the size of your class.

- Cut out the puzzle pieces from Reproducible 3E. Laminate the pieces, if possible.

- Place each set of laminated pieces in a shallow container filled with play sand or pebbles. The kids in your class will enjoy taking turns pulling the pieces out of the container and putting the verse in the correct order.

- You may choose to group younger and older kids together. Younger kids may enjoy finding the puzzle pieces. Older kids may enjoy figuring out the correct order for the verse.

- Instruct the kids to refer to the Unit 1 Bible Verse Poster (Class Pack—pp. 10 & 15) to put the puzzle pieces in order.

SAY: Our Bible verse says, "But forgiveness is with you—that's why you are honored" (Psalm 130:4). We will learn more about how forgiveness is a big part of Joseph's story this month.

Tip: Save this activity to use again next week.

Peaceful Place

Supplies: Celebrate Wonder Bible Storybook, suggested book: "I Love My New Toy!" by Mo Willems, seven cows and seven grains (pictures or toys), containers with different grains, glue, paper, sand tray

- Assist the children, as needed, as they interact with the items provided.

- Let the children feel the grains and glue the grains on paper to make a picture.

Tip: All of the supplies/activities suggested for the Peaceful Place are optional. Choose what you want or add your own ideas.

Go in Peace

Spiritual Practice – Exploring Reconciliation Through Forgiveness

Supplies: bottle of bubbles with wand

SAY: A spiritual practice is something we do to help us connect to God. Reconciling with and forgiving others helps us grow closer to God. It can be hard to forgive others when we have been hurt, but that is what God wants us to do. God always forgives us, no matter what we do

- Guide the children through this spiritual practice:
  - ○ Have the children stand in a circle and close their eyes. Have them each think of someone who has hurt them.
  - ○ Give the bubbles to the first child.

SAY: Blow a bubble. As the bubble drifts away, say, "I am forgiven, so I forgive."

- Have the children pass around the bubbles, so everyone has a chance to forgive.

PRAY: Repeat after me: "God, I am thankful you forgive me. Help me to forgive others. Amen."

- Bless the children before they leave. Touch each child as you say this blessing: "May you always carry forgiveness in your heart. God bless you."

Family Spiritual Practice

SAY: Let's take a look at your Take-Home Pages for today (*Reproducibles 3F–3G*). Ask your family to participate in this week's spiritual practice.

Supplemental Activities

Preschoolers – Retell the Story with Song

- Have the children interact with the Unit 1 Bible story figures (Class Pack—p. 6) as you sing the song.
- Sing the verse to the tune of "The Farmer in the Dell."

SING: Oh, Joseph helped the pharaoh. / Oh, Joseph helped the pharaoh. / Pharaoh asked for Joseph's help. / And Joseph helped the pharaoh.

SAY: After Joseph was in prison for thirteen years, the pharaoh finally freed him. Joseph could have been mad at the pharaoh, but he helped him instead. It didn't take Joseph long to forgive the pharaoh.

WONDER: Do you think Joseph thought about his brothers? Do you think he would forgive them?

Early and Older Elementary – Gather and Save

Supplies: two small buckets for each team, spoons, beads or gems, masking tape, timer

Prepare Ahead: Use masking tape to create a start line and a finish line for each team. Place a bucket with beads at the start line for each team (buckets should have fairly even amounts) and an empty bucket at the finish line for each team.

SAY: In the Bible story, Joseph interpreted Pharaoh's dream that there would be seven years of good harvest and seven years of famine. So, Joseph knew they needed to save grain while they could. Let's play a gather-and-save relay race.

- Split the children into teams and have each team line up at its start line.

- Give the first child in each team a spoon.

- Have the child use the spoon to get a scoop of beads, carry them to the finish line, pour them into the empty bucket, and return to the start to give the spoon to the next child on the team.

- Set a timer for five minutes.

- Make sure the children are lined up in their places. Then count back from five, start the timer, and say, "Go." The team with the highest level of beads or gems in their finish line bucket, wins.

Intergenerational Activity – Food Collection

- This week work on the food drive for your church that you may have started last week.

- If you haven't done so already, make photocopies of Reproducible 2E and hand them out to your class and to other members of the church.

- Plan how the food drive will work. For example, you might invite church members to bring food donations to your church building for the next few weeks. Then decide if a food pantry or other group will receive your donations.

- There are different ways you may choose to organize the food drive donations:

  ❍ Divide the kids, youth, and adults into several groups. Invite the groups to sort the items into similar categories.

  ❍ Have your class sort the items. Then have youth and adult volunteers deliver the items to a local food pantry.

  ❍ If you have a food pantry in your church, teams of volunteers can work together to bring the items to the pantry.

But forgiveness is with you—that's why you are honored. (Psalm 130:4)

Joseph and His Brothers Reunited – Genesis 42:1–46:34

Prepare to Wonder

Faith Word: Reconciliation

The seven years of plenty and the seven years of famine arrived, just as Pharaoh's dream had predicted. Joseph took good care of the grains during the seven years of plenty, so the Egyptian people had food to eat during the seven years of famine. Egypt was not the only country affected by the drought. Canaan, where Joseph's father and brothers lived, also had a famine. Jacob sent his sons to Egypt to buy food so they wouldn't starve to death.

When the brothers arrived in Egypt, they were taken to their brother, Joseph, to request food (although, of course, they did not know it was him). It had been many years since the brothers had seen Joseph, and they did not recognize him. But Joseph *did* recognize his brothers. Joseph devised a plan to trick his brothers and get even for selling him. Joseph wanted them to feel remorse for what they did to him.

Joseph finally decided he could not trick his brothers any longer and revealed himself to his brothers. He was so overcome by emotion, he had to hide his tears. Joseph forgave his brothers and wanted to be reconciled with them and his father. Joseph sent his brothers back to Canaan one last time. They returned with their father and the rest of the family to make Egypt their home. The family was reunited.

Forgiveness can take a long time. It may take years to work through the process of reconciling. In the story of Joseph and his brothers, reconciliation was achieved because both sides asked for and gave forgiveness.

Spiritual Practice for Adults

Have you been in a situation where peace needed to be restored? How did you restore peace? When you are confronted with conflict this week practice the three *S's*: **Stop** before you speak, **Speak** with words of kindness, and sincerely **Say** you are sorry.

Come Together

Come Together

Supplies: Class Pack, Celebrate Wonder Bible Storybook, a paper heart cut in half, green cloth, battery-operated candle

Prepare Ahead: Set up a Wonder Table (see p. 3) with a green cloth, battery-operated candle, and a Wonder Box (see p. 3). Display the Unit 1 Bible Verse Poster (Class Pack—pp. 10 & 15) and Faith Word Poster (Class Pack—p. 4). Place a heart cut in half inside the Wonder Box.

- Point to the Unit 1 Faith Word Poster, and invite the children to wonder about what the word *reconciliation* means.

- Invite the kids to join you in a circle.

SAY: Our story today is about how Joseph got to see his brothers again.

- Take a few minutes to talk about last week's Bible story.

- We recommend reading a story from the *Celebrate Wonder Bible Storybook.* Allow an elementary kid to read, "Joseph and His Brothers Reunited" (pp. 48–49), from the storybook.

PRAY: Dear God, Joseph forgave his brothers. Help us forgive others too. Amen.

Coin Rubbings – Preschool

Supplies: Reproducible Kids' Book, pennies or other coins, crayons

Prepare Ahead: Photocopy Reproducible 4A for each preschooler.

- Invite elementary kids to help the preschoolers place coins under their reproducible sheet and use crayons to make crayon rubbings.

SAY: In today's Bible story, Joseph's brothers came to Egypt to get food. They brought silver with them to give as a gift.

The Brothers Travel to Egypt – Younger Elementary

Supplies: Reproducible Kids' Book, crayons, pencils

Prepare Ahead: Photocopy "The Brothers Travel to Egypt" (Reproducible 4B) for each child.

SAY: Help Joseph's brothers get to Egypt.

- Invite the kids to work out the solution to the maze on Reproducible 4B.

ASK: Today we will hear more about how Joseph and his brothers reunited after many, many years.

- Invite the kids to color the picture.

Paper Pyramids – Older Elementary

Supplies: Reproducible Kids' Book, scissors, tape, markers

Supplies: Photocopy Reproducibles 4C and 4D for each child.

- Invite the kids to cut out the large outer square from "Paper Pyramid" (Reproducible 4C). The four smaller squares or quadrants should not be cut.
- Invite the kids to use copies of "Paper Pyramid Instructions" (Reproducible 4D) to learn how to fold the paper square from Reproducible 4C into pyramids.

SAY: This month we have heard stories about Joseph and his time in Egypt. Today we are learning how Joseph forgave his brothers.

- Once the paper pyramids have been folded, invite the kids to secure their pyramids with a small piece of tape.
- Invite them to write *I can forgive others* on one or more sides of their pyramids using a marker.

Sticky Hearts – All Ages

Supplies: paper heart cut in half, contact paper, tissue paper, hole punch, yarn, tape, scissors

Prepare Ahead: Cut the contact paper into a heart shape, one for each child. Punch a hole in the top of each contact paper heart. Cut tissue paper into one-inch squares. Cut yarn into six-inch pieces, one for each child.

SAY: There are many ways to experience reconciliation. Reconciliation is like bringing two pieces of a heart together.

- Show the children the paper heart cut in two. Tape the two pieces together to complete the heart.

SAY: Hearts can be put back together when you forgive.

- Peel off the paper from the contact paper heart for each child.
- Invite each child to place the tissue paper on the sticky side of the heart.
- Tie the yarn through the hole in the top of the heart.

WONDER: How do you think God feels when you forgive someone?

Wonder Time

Interactive Bible Story

Supplies: Reproducible Kids' Book

Prepare Ahead: Photocopy today's Take-Home Pages from the Reproducible Kids' Book, 4F–4G (pp. 77–78). "Joseph and His Brother Reunited" is written in short sections that are one to three sentences long. Display the Unit 1 Bible Verse Poster (Class Pack—pp. 10 & 15).

- Invite several readers to take turns reading the story one section at a time.
- Read through the story.

SAY: Joseph's story had lots of ups and downs! God helped Joseph find the strength to forgive his brothers. As a result, Joseph and his brothers came back together as a family.

Share a Story

Supplies: Celebrate Wonder DVD, TV, DVD player

- Invite the children to join you, sitting in a circle on the floor.
- Watch the Session 4 video (Celebrate Wonder DVD).

Wonder with Me

Supplies: Class Pack, Wonder Box, scissors

Prepare Ahead: Lay out the Unit 1 Wonder Story Mat (Class Pack—pp. 7 & 18). Cut out the final Unit 1 story figure of Jacob, Joseph's father (Class Pack—p. 6), if not already done.

- Place the Wonder Box on the Unit 1 Wonder Story Mat.

SAY: We have heard many Bible stories about the Faith Word, *reconciliation*.

- Show the children the Unit 1 Faith Word Poster (Class Pack—p. 4).

SAY: *Reconciliation* means to bring peace between persons who have disagreed.

- Point to the words on the Wonder Story Mat.

SAY: This word is *reconciliation,* which means to bring peace to people who disagree. This word is *forgiveness.* You forgive so you can be reconciled and stay friends.

WONDER together:

- ❍ What might have happened if Joseph had tricked his brothers?
- ❍ Do you think Joseph and his brothers could have reconciled—become friends again—if Joseph tricked them?

- Place the Bible story figure of Jacob on the Wonder Story Mat.
- Open the Wonder Box to reveal the "broken" heart.

WONDER: Do you think Joseph's heart was broken when his brothers hurt him? How do you think Joseph's heart felt when he reconciled with his brothers?

Experience Wonder

What Am I Feeling?

Supplies: posterboard or large sheet of paper, marker

- Put the kids in pairs. If possible, pair a younger kid with an older kid.

SAY: This month we have been learning how Joseph's brothers treated him badly.

ASK: What did Joseph's brothers do?

- Take a moment to review the beginning of Joseph's story. Joseph was the favorite son of Jacob. As a result, the brothers treated Joseph horribly.

SAY: Sometimes it can be hard to understand why people do what they do. Maybe Joseph wondered why his brothers had been so mean to him.

- On the posterboard, write down all the emotions the class can think of (happiness, sadness, anger, fear, surprise, jealousy, and so forth).
- Play a game in pairs. In this game, have the kids take turns making different expressions. Have the partners guess what emotion is being acted out.

SAY: When we try to understand how someone else feels, that can make us feel compassion for others. Maybe Joseph could forgive his brothers because he understood how they must have felt.

Examine the Bible Verse

SAY: Our Unit 1 Bible verse is Psalm 130:4. Find it in your Bibles.

ASK: Is the Book of Psalms in the Old or New Testament? *(Old)* Where is Psalms located in the Old Testament? *(about the middle of your Bible)* In what chapter of Psalms is our verse located? *(130)* What is the verse number? *(4)*

- Gather the kids around the Unit 1 Bible Verse Poster. Read it together.

ASK: What is the reference for our verse? *(Psalm 130:4)*

SAY: Our Bible verse helps us understand that forgiveness comes from God. We will learn about forgiveness and reconciliation as we hear more about Joseph's story.

Peaceful Place

Supplies: Celebrate Wonder Bible Storybook, suggested book: "Molly & Mae: A Friendship Journey" by Danny Parker and Freya Blackwood, grain containers to sort, two-piece heart puzzles, paper, crayons or markers

- Assist the children, as needed, as they interact with the items provided.

- Have the children sort the grain and match the hearts.

- Give each child paper, and have each child draw a picture of her or his family.

Tip: All of the supplies/activities suggested for the Peaceful Place are optional.

Go in Peace

Spiritual Practice – Exploring Reconciliation Through Forgiveness

SAY: Spiritual practice is something we do to help us connect to God. It doesn't have to be the same spiritual practice all the time, but it can be. There is no right or wrong way to do spiritual practice. This week we will practice what we should do to keep peace between persons who might disagree. Think of the three *S's.*

- Guide the children through spiritual practice:

  ○ **Stop** before you speak and think about what you will say or do. *(Hold your hand out in a stop motion.)*

  ○ **Speak** in words of kindness. *(Cup your hand around your mouth.)*

  ○ **Say** you are sorry if you were wrong. *(Hold out your hand.)*

PRAY: Repeat after me: "God, help me be a messenger of forgiveness and reconciliation. Amen."

- Bless the children before they leave. Touch each child as you say this blessing: "May you always carry forgiveness in your heart. God bless you."

Family Spiritual Practice

SAY: Let's take a look at your Take-Home Pages for today *(Reproducibles 4F–4G).* Ask your family to participate in this week's spiritual practice.

Supplemental Activities

Preschoolers – Retell the Story with Song

SAY: We are going to learn the last verse to the Joseph song.

- Have the children interact with the Unit 1 Bible story figures (Class Pack—p. 6) as you sing the song.

- Sing the verse to the tune of "The Farmer in the Dell."

SING: Oh, Joseph shared the food. His brothers, Joseph loved. / Oh, Joseph shared the food. His brothers, Joseph loved. / His brothers came to buy some food; they brought their father to Egypt. / And Joseph shared the food. His brothers, Joseph loved.

WONDER: What part of Joseph's story did you like the best? What part didn't you like? What is something you learned from the story?

Early Elementary – Find the Missing Piece

Supplies: Reproducible Kids' Book, scissors, letter-size envelopes

Prepare Ahead: Photocopy "Joseph and His Brothers Reunited" (Reproducible 4G) for each child. For each child, cut out the pieces and place in an envelope. Then remove one piece from each envelope, and hide the pieces around the room.

SAY: Sometimes conflict makes us feels like we are broken into pieces or something is missing. God helps us put our pieces back together when we experience reconciliation.

- Give each child an envelope of heart puzzle pieces. Do not tell them that they each have a missing piece.

- Invite the children to put their heart puzzles together. Give them time to realize they are all missing a piece.

- Encourage the children to search around the classroom for their missing pieces. As each child finds a piece, have him or her see if the piece completes the puzzle. If the piece belongs to someone else's puzzle, encourage the child to find the person who needs the found piece.

Older Elementary – Beach Ball Review

Supplies: beach ball, Sharpie marker, painters' tape

Prepare Ahead: Write the review questions on strips of painters' tape and place them around on the beach ball before today's session.

- Gather the children in a circle wide enough to allow space to either toss or roll the ball between one another. Wherever the child's left thumb lands is the question they will answer.

Review Questions:

1. What animals were in Pharaoh's dream?
2. What is our unit memory verse?
3. How many years did they have famine in Egypt?
4. How many brothers did Joseph have?
5. What does *reconciliation* mean?
6. What was the name of Joseph's youngest brother?
7. What was your favorite activity we did the past four weeks?
8. What is something new you learned about the story of Joseph?

Intergenerational Activity – Food Collection

Supplies: Reproducible Kids' Book; cookie-making ingredients and supplies as listed on Reproducible 4E; napkins; disposable plates; optional: milk, disposable cups

Prepare Ahead: Photocopy "Oatmeal Cookies" (Reproducible 4E) for each group.

Tip: Check for food allergies prior to the start of this activity.

- Put the kids, youth, and adults into groups who can work together to make cookies. Be sure each group has a mix of kids, youth, and adults.

SAY: We've been learning about the life of Joseph and his brothers. When there was no food in the land, Jacob sent his sons to Egypt to buy grain. Grain is found in lots of foods we enjoy, even cookies!

- Hand out copies of Reproducible 4E and supplies to each group.

- Invite the adults in each group to give the kids and youth instructions for making the cookies.

- While the cookies are baking, kids, youth, and adults may do other activities.

- Ask a volunteer or multiple volunteers to keep an eye on the cookies as they bake.

- You may plan to have the groups come back together after Sunday school or worship to enjoy their cookies. Or you may choose to have groups bag up the cookies and give them to someone special in your church or community.

The people were in awe of the LORD, and they believed in the LORD and in his servant Moses. (Exodus 14:31b)

The Baby in the Basket – Exodus 1:8-14; 2:1-10

Prepare to Wonder

Faith Word: Awe

At the end of Unit 1, Joseph had invited all of his family to come and live in Egypt, where food was plentiful. They left Canaan and moved to Egypt, where they grew in number. But times change—Joseph died and new pharaohs came to power. In this unit, we pick up the story of the Israelites about four hundred years after Joseph.

A new pharaoh had come to power in Egypt, and he was afraid of the Israelites because their number was so large. He fears the Israelites will overtake the Egyptians and claim power from the pharaoh. After many attempts to control the population of the Israelites, the pharaoh finally enslaves them. When enslaving doesn't work, he gives the order to kill any male baby born to an Israelite woman.

This is the world Moses is born in. Moses is the baby of Israelite parents and could be killed if discovered. When Moses was too big to hide, his mother placed him in a basket and hid him among the reeds of the river. In a remarkable twist, the pharaoh's daughter found Moses and adopted him as her own, knowing he was an Israelite. How awe-inspiring is it that Moses, an Israelite baby, was saved by an Egyptian pharaoh's daughter and that baby would end up saving the Israelites and leading them out of slavery!

Spiritual Practice for Adults

In this unit, we will explore awe through gratitude. I can imagine the feelings of gratitude the mother of Moses had for the pharaoh's daughter for saving her baby. Sit in a comfortable position and close your eyes. Imagine you are sitting beside a river that is flowing slowly. Think of the many blessings God has given you as the water slowly moves by. Give thanks to God for all you have been given and all you are thankful for.

Come Together

Come Together

Supplies: Class Pack, Celebrate Wonder Bible Storybook, Wonder Box, green cloth, battery-operated candle, basket

Prepare Ahead: Set up a Wonder Table (see p. 3) with a green cloth, battery-operated candle, and a Wonder Box (see p. 3). Display the Unit 2 Bible Verse Poster (Class Pack—pp. 12 & 13) and Faith Word Poster (Class Pack—21). Place the basket inside the Wonder Box.

- Point to the Unit 2 Faith Word Poster, and invite the children to wonder about what the word *awe* means.
- Invite the kids to join you in a circle.

SAY: This month we are hearing stories about a man named Moses. Our story today starts when Moses was just a little baby.

- We recommend reading a story from the *Celebrate Wonder Bible Storybook*. Allow an elementary kid to read, "The Baby in the Basket" (pp. 50–51), from the storybook.

PRAY: Dear God, thank you for taking care of baby Moses. Thank you for taking care of me! Amen.

Baby in a Basket – Preschool

Supplies: Reproducible Kids' Book, crayons or markers

- Give each preschooler a photocopy of "Baby in a Basket" (Reproducible 5A) and invite each child to connect the dots. Then have the preschoolers color the picture.

SAY: In today's Bible story, Moses' sister watched over him as he floated in a basket.

Baby Moses Maze – Younger Elementary

Supplies: Reproducible Kids' Book, crayons or markers

- Hand out a photocopy of "Baby Moses Maze" (Reproducible 5B) to each kid.

SAY: Help baby Moses' basket *(at the top of the page)* find its way to Pharaoh's daughter *(at the bottom of the page)*.

- Invite the kids to work through the maze on the page.

ASK: Why was baby Moses put in a basket? Why did Moses' mother put the basket in the river?

- Invite the kids to share their predictions about today's Bible story.

Backwards Bible Verse – Older Elementary

Supplies: Reproducible Kids' Book, pencils

- Hand out a photocopy of "Backwards Bible Verse" (Reproducible 5C) to each kid.

SAY: The Bible verse for this month has been written backwards. To decode the verse, begin at the BOTTOM of the page and rewrite each word by putting the letters in the correct order. Then rewrite the entire verse in the box at the bottom of the page.

- Invite older-elementary kids to work on "Backwards Bible Verse" from Reproducible 5C. Help them as needed.

- Have the kids share the Bible verse once they have rewritten it at the bottom of the page.

Stars and Constellations – All Ages

Supplies: Reproducible Kids' Book, crayons or markers

Prepare Ahead: Make a photocopy of "September Stars and Constellations" (Reproducible 1D) and "October Stars and Constellations" (Reproducible 5D) for each kid in your class.

- Invite the kids to place both reproducible sheets in front of them on the table. Have them place the September sheet (Reproducible 1D) on the left and the October sheet (Reproducible 5D) on the right.

SAY: This fall, we are learning about stars and constellations. Look at the two sheets. The first sheet is from September. The second sheet is from October. Can you find the stars and constellations found on both of the sheets?

- Invite the kids to work together to find which stars and constellations appear on both sheets. Have the kids circle those star pictures on both sheets.

SAY: Stars move across the sky throughout the night. Each night, the star pictures change just a little bit. Next month, we'll get a new star chart. You'll see some old star pictures and some new star pictures.

- Invite the kids to take the sheets home and look at the sky!

SAY: Looking at stars gives me a sense of awe and wonder.

Wonder Time

Interactive Bible Story

Supplies: *Reproducible Kids' Book*

Prepare Ahead: *Photocopy the Take-Home Pages from the Reproducible Kids' Book, 5F–5G (pp. 79–80).*

- "The Baby in the Basket" is written in short sections that are one to three sentences long. Invite several readers to take turns reading the story one section at a time.

- Read through the story.

SAY: Moses' mother cared for him. God cared for Moses too.

- Read the story a second time, if time allows.

Share a Story

Supplies: *Celebrate Wonder DVD, TV, DVD player*

- Invite the children to join you, sitting in a circle on the floor.

- Watch the Session 5 video (Celebrate Wonder DVD).

Wonder with Me

Supplies: *Class Pack, Wonder Box, scissors*

Prepare Ahead: *Lay out the Unit 2 Wonder Story Mat (Class Pack—pp. 8 & 17). Cut out the five Unit 2 Bible story figures (Class Pack—p. 19).*

- Place the Wonder Box on the Unit 2 Wonder Story Mat.

SAY: *Awe is the Faith Word for this unit.*

- Show the children the Unit 2 Faith Word Poster (Class Pack—p. 21).

SAY: The definition of *awe* is an amazing feeling of wonder inspired by God.

SAY: The story of Moses is a long one and takes Moses to many places on an awe-inspiring journey. We will chart Moses' journey on the timeline, starting with Moses as a baby.

WONDER together:

  ○ Why do you think the pharaoh's daughter took Moses out of the river?

  ○ What do you think will happen to Moses next?

  ○ How do you think it felt to float in the river in a basket?

- Place the Unit 2 Bible story figure of baby Moses in a basket on the matching circle at the bottom of the Unit 2 Wonder Story Mat timeline.

- Open the Wonder Box to reveal the basket.

WONDER: How does a basket fit into the Bible story?

Experience Wonder

What Floats?

Supplies: large bin, water, plastic table cover, large towel, small baskets, plastic boats, assorted objects that may or may not float, aluminum foil, scissors

Prepare Ahead: Place the plastic cover on the table and place the large towel over it. Fill the bin with water and place on the large towel. Cut the aluminum foil into twelve-inch squares of aluminum foil.

- Give each child a piece of aluminum foil. Have them make something out of the foil that they think will float.

- Let the children experiment with the objects to find out which ones float and which ones don't.

SAY: Baby Moses was placed in a basket and put in the river. The mother of Moses made sure the basket would float by sealing it with tar. She asked Moses' sister, Miriam, to hide in the reeds and watch over her brother.

WONDER: Why do you think Moses' mother wanted to make sure the basket floated before she put Moses in the river? Why was it important for Miriam to watch over Moses?

Examine the Bible Verse

SAY: Our Unit 2 Bible verse is Exodus 14:31b. Find it in your Bibles.

ASK: Is the Book of Exodus in the Old or New Testament? *(Old)* Where is Exodus located in the Old Testament? *(second book)* What is the chapter number? *(14)* What is the verse number? *(31b)*

- Gather the kids around the Unit 2 Bible Verse Poster (Class Pack—pp. 12 & 13). Read it together.

ASK: What is the reference for our verse? *(Exodus 14:31b)*

Peaceful Place

Supplies: Leader Guide—p. 114; Celebrate Wonder Bible Storybook; suggested book: "Thank You, God, for Everything: A Nursery Rhyme Picture Book" by Karen Marie Graham; baby dolls, baskets, baby blankets; paper; crayons or markers

Prepare Ahead: Photocopy the Unit 2 Faith Word coloring sheet (Leader Guide—p. 114) for each child. Make extra copies of the Unit 2 Faith Word coloring sheet to leave in the Peaceful Place.

- Assist the children, as needed, as they interact with the items provided.
- Give each child a piece of paper, and have the children draw a picture of things Miriam may have seen or heard as she watched over baby Moses.
- Let each child color the Awe Faith Word sheet.

Tip: All of the supplies/activities suggested for the Peaceful Place are optional.

Go in Peace

Spiritual Practice – Exploring Awe Through Gratitude

Supplies: Leader Guide—pp. 111, 112; index cards; crayons or markers

SAY: Spiritual practice is something we do to help us connect to God. This week the Bible story is about a mother who loved her baby so much, she put him in a basket in the river, hoping he would be saved. She was probably surprised and filled with awe and gratitude when the pharaoh's daughter found him.

- Guide the children through a spiritual practice:

SAY: What fills you with gratitude? Draw a picture of what fills you with gratitude on an index card.

PRAY: Repeat after me: "Thank you, God, for filling us with gratitude. Amen."

- Bless the children before they leave. Touch each child as you say this blessing: "May you always find something to be grateful for. God bless you."
- Send home a photocopy of the Celebration Chart (Leader Guide—p. 111) and the Family Letter (Leader Guide—p. 112) with any child who does not already have one.

Family Spiritual Practice

SAY: Let's take a look at your Take-Home Pages for today *(Reproducibles 5F–5G)*. Ask your family to participate in this week's spiritual practice.

Supplemental Activities

Preschoolers – Cover Baby Moses

Supplies: drawing paper, torn-up pieces of construction paper, glue, crayons or markers

- Give each child drawing paper, and have each child draw a picture of baby Moses.

- When they are done drawing baby Moses, have them glue the torn-up pieces of construction paper over or around Moses to hide him.

SAY: Moses' mother wanted to make sure Moses was safe in the river. She hid him in the reeds along the river, but still made sure he could be seen by his sister, Miriam.

WONDER: Who wants to make sure you are safe? Why did Moses' mother want to make sure he stayed safe?

Early Elementary – Baby Inclusion Inspectors

Supplies: clipboards (can be pretend and made from cardboard), paper, pencils, optional: dress-up items for the kids to use to look "official"

SAY: It is important that our church is a place where every person is welcome and feels like they belong. One way we make people feel welcome is to make sure our environment is safe and there are lots of ways for people to participate.

ASK: What kinds of things has our church done to help keep you safe and make you feel welcome? How does our church include you?

SAY: Today we are going to pretend to be "Baby Inclusion Inspectors." We are going to take a walk and look around our church. We are going to play close attention to the ways we are keeping babies safe, including them, and making them feel welcome.

- Give each child a piece of paper, a clipboard, and a pencil.

- Take a walk around and through the church together. Encourage the children to write down or draw what they see on the paper on their clipboards.

- Return to the classroom and invite any children who would like to share to show the group their drawings and lists.

- With the children's permission, share their findings with the pastor or another person in church leadership.

Older Elementary – Courage to Care

Supplies: paper, colored pencils or fine-tip markers, pencils

SAY: What do you think it takes to show courage? How do you feel when you do something hard because you care for someone?

- Guide the children to create their own courageous caring stories by drawing a comic strip. Allow time and creative art supplies for them to imagine and work.

- Or they can share an experience they have had personally.

- Allow time to share these as a group when you are ready.

Intergenerational Activity – Caring for Babies

Prepare Ahead: If your church family has babies and a nursery, coordinate with the nursery coordinator to have your class and adult volunteers care for the babies together. If you do not have a church nursery, invite parents who have a baby to visit your class. Interacting with a real baby will help the kids in your class understand the way Moses' mother made a decision to save her son.

- After the kids have had an interaction with babies using one of the two ideas above, gather the group together and discuss their experience.

- Ask questions about taking care of babies or playing with babies. They may also share about babies they know, like siblings or cousins or grandbabies.

SAY: In today's Bible story, we heard how Moses' mother put her baby in a basket and placed him in the river.

ASK: Do you think that would have been a difficult thing for Moses' mother to do? Why do you think she did it?

- Invite the kids to reflect on today's Bible story and think about why baby Moses was placed in a basket.

SAY: Moses' mother wanted to save her baby! God was watching out for baby Moses. God watches out for us.

The people were in awe of the LORD, and they believed in the LORD and in his servant Moses. (Exodus 14:31b)

God Speaks to Moses – Exodus 3:1-22

Prepare to Wonder

Faith Word: Awe

Moses is now a grown man. He has led a privileged life as the grandson of the pharaoh, but Moses knows he is an Israelite. The mistreatment of his people, the Israelites, upsets Moses and he ends up killing an Egyptian for mistreating an Israelite slave. He flees to Midian, where he marries and becomes a shepherd.

One day while Moses is tending his sheep, he comes across a burning bush. Moses was amazed because the bush was burning, but it was not being consumed. As Moses moved closer, he heard a voice. The voice said, "I am the God of your father, Abraham's God, Isaac's God, and Jacob's God" (Exodus 3:6).

God called Moses to return to Egypt and rescue his people from slavery. Moses didn't think he was the man for the job. After all, he didn't speak very well. God wasn't going to allow Moses to get out of going to Egypt. God sent Aaron, his brother, with him to help him speak.

Moses was afraid. Most of us feel that way when we are called to do something we don't think we are prepared to do. God promised Moses to go with him, and Moses trusted God. With God's help, Moses returned to Egypt to free his people and start a journey that would last many years. We may not hear God's voice in a burning bush today, but we can hear it and see it in the expressions of gratitude.

Spiritual Practice for Adults

Sit comfortably, close your eyes, and imagine you are standing in front of a bush that is burning but not being consumed. Remove your shoes and know you are on holy ground. What is God calling you to do? Are you hesitant to follow God's calling? The journey may be long, but you will experience many awesome moments and be filled with gratitude along the way. God will be with you.

Come Together

Come Together

Supplies: Class Pack, Celebrate Wonder Bible Storybook, Wonder Box, green cloth, battery-operated candle, second battery-operated candle

Prepare Ahead: Set up a Wonder Table (see p. 3) with a green cloth, battery-operated candle, and a Wonder Box (see p. 3). Display the Unit 2 Bible Verse Poster (Class Pack—pp. 12 & 13) and Faith Word Poster (Class Pack—p. 21). Place the other candle inside the Wonder Box.

- Point to the Unit 2 Faith Word Poster, and invite the children to wonder about what the word *awe* means.
- Invite the kids to join you in a circle.

SAY: This month we are hearing stories about a man named Moses. Our story today tells us what happened when God met with Moses.

- Take a few minutes to talk about last week's Bible story.
- We recommend reading a story from the *Celebrate Wonder Bible Storybook.* Allow an elementary kid to read, "God Speaks to Moses" (pp. 52–53), from the storybook.

PRAY: Dear God, thank you for meeting with Moses. Thank you that we can meet with you in times of worship, learning, and prayer. Amen.

God Speaks to Moses – Preschool

Supplies: Reproducible Kids' Book, crayons or markers

- Give each preschooler a photocopy of "God Speaks to Moses" (Reproducible 6A), and invite them to color the picture.

SAY: In today's Bible story, God met with Moses. God wanted to help the Hebrew people. They were in trouble.

Burning Bush – Younger Elementary

Supplies: Reproducible Kids' Book, white card stock, watercolor paints, paintbrushes, cups of water, colored pencils, smocks, paper towels

- Photocopy "Burning Bush" (Reproducible 6B) onto white card stock, one for each child.

- Put watercolor paints, brushes, and cups of water on the table. Have paper towels handy.

- Hand out the card-stock copies of Reproducible 6B to the kids.

SAY: In today's Bible story, Moses met God! God appeared to Moses in a flaming bush that did not burn up.

- Invite the kids to put their names on the page.

- Have them follow the directions on the page to color the bush with colored pencils.

- Then invite the kids to paint flames of fire coming from the bush in the picture using watercolors.

SAY: In today's Bible story, God appeared to Moses in the flames of a fire. We will learn more as we hear the story.

Pixel Art – Older Elementary

Supplies: *Reproducible Kids' Book, colored pencils (orange, brown, yellow)*

- Hand out a photocopy of "Pixel Art" (Reproducible 6C) to each kid.

SAY: God spoke to Moses in a dramatic way. To find out how God spoke to Moses, color by number on the page. Color according to these directions: 1 = Orange, 2 = Brown, 3 = Yellow.

- Invite older-elementary kids to work together to figure out how to color in the picture using the colored pencils.

- Help the kids as necessary.

Shoes-Off Game – All Ages

Supplies: *roll of masking tape*

Prepare Ahead: *Use masking tape to mark a starting line at one end of the classroom. At the other end of the classroom, use masking tape to mark a finish line. Make sure there is some space between the classroom wall and the finish line, where the kids will pile up their shoes.*

- Invite the kids to remove their shoes and make a big pile of shoes between the classroom wall and the finish line.

- Divide the kids into two teams, and have them form two lines behind the starting line.

SAY: In today's Bible story, God meets with Moses. God appears to Moses in a flame of fire on a bush. When God speaks, God tells Moses to take off his shoes.

- When you say, "Go," one member from each team should move to the pile of shoes. When they get there, the kids should find their shoes in the pile and put them back on. Then the kids should move back to their team.

- Invite the next kid from each team to follow the same directions, until each team has retrieved their shoes.

- Instruct the kids that the pile of shoes should remain behind the finish line. In other words, no throwing others' shoes around the room! If a team breaks the rule, they lose automatically.

- See which team is able to retrieve their shoes first.

SAY: I wonder why God wanted Moses to remove his shoes.

Wonder Time

Interactive Bible Story

Supplies: Reproducible Kids' Book

Prepare Ahead: Photocopy the Take-Home Pages from the Reproducible Kids' Book, 6F–6G (pp. 81–82).

- "God Speaks to Moses" is written in short sections that are one to three sentences long. Invite several readers to take turns reading the story one section at a time.

- Read through the story.

SAY: God spoke to Moses. God had a job for Moses to do.

- Read the story a second time, if time allows.

Share a Story

Supplies: Celebrate Wonder DVD, TV, DVD player

- Invite the children to join you, sitting in a circle on the floor.

- Watch the Session 6 video (Celebrate Wonder DVD).

Wonder with Me

Supplies: Class Pack, Wonder Box, tape, scissors

Prepare Ahead: Lay out the Unit 2 Wonder Story Mat (Class Pack—pp. 8 & 17). Cut out the four remaining Unit 2 Bible story figures (Class Pack—p. 19), if not done already.

- Place the Wonder Box on the Unit 2 Wonder Story Mat.

- Show the children the Unit 2 Faith Word Poster (Class Pack—p. 21).

SAY: The definition of *awe* is an amazing feeling of wonder inspired by God.

SAY: In this unit, we are talking about awe being an amazing feeling of wonder inspired by God.

- Point to the blank spaces on the timeline on the Unit 2 Wonder Story Mat.

WONDER together:

- ❍ What inspires awe in you when you hear the Bible story today?
- ❍ What do you wonder about in the Bible story?
- ❍ How might God talk to us today?

- Place the Bible story figure of Moses before the burning bush on the square above Moses in the basket on the Unit 2 Wonder Story Mat timeline.

- Open the Wonder Box to reveal the candle.

WONDER: Why is there a candle in the Wonder Box?

Experience Wonder

3D Burning Bush

Supplies: black construction paper; raffia; red, yellow, and orange puff paints; glue, smocks; scissors, paintbrushes

Prepare Ahead: Cut raffia into six-inch pieces.

- Give each child a piece of black construction paper.
- Show the children how to glue the raffia on the paper and drop the puff paints around the raffia to create a burning bush.

SAY: God chose the burning bush to talk to Moses. God had something very important to tell Moses, and God wanted Moses' full attention. Moses was curious about the burning bush because it was burning but not being burned up.

WONDER: Do you think Moses was in awe when he saw the bush in flames? I wonder how Moses felt when God's voice came from the bush. How would you feel?

Examine the Bible Verse

SAY: Our Unit 2 Bible verse is Exodus 14:31b. Find it in your Bibles.

ASK: Is the Book of Exodus in the Old or New Testament? *(Old)* Where is Exodus located in the Old Testament? *(second book)* What is the chapter number? *(14)* What is the verse number? *(31b)*

- Gather the kids around the Unit 2 Bible Verse Poster (Class Pack—pp. 12 & 13) Read it together.

ASK: What is the reference for our verse? *(Exodus 14:31b)*

Peaceful Place

Supplies: Celebrate Wonder Bible Storybook, suggested book: "Tree: A Peek-Through Picture Book" by Britta Teckentrup, interlocking blocks, candle from the Wonder Box, paper, crayons or markers

- Assist the children, as needed, as they interact with the items provided.
- Invite the children to draw a picture of what inspires awe and wonder in them.

Tip: All of the supplies/activities suggested for the Peaceful Place are optional.

Go in Peace

Spiritual Practice – Exploring Awe Through Gratitude

Supplies: Leader Guide—p. 111, candle from the Peaceful Place/Wonder Box, index cards, crayons or markers

SAY: Spiritual practice is something we do to help us connect to God. It doesn't have to be the same spiritual practice all the time, but it can be. There is no right or wrong way to do spiritual practice. Connecting to God is the most important reason to do a spiritual practice. This week we talked about the awe and wonder of God speaking to Moses through the burning bush.

- Turn the candle on and guide the children through a spiritual practice.

SAY: What are you thankful that you learned today?

SAY: Draw a picture of what you learned today on an index card.

PRAY: Repeat after me: "Thank you, God, for teaching us to be thankful. Amen."

- Bless the children before they leave. Touch each child as you say this blessing: "May you always be filled with awe and gratitude for God's wonderful world."
- Send home a photocopy of the Celebration Chart (Leader Guide—p. 111) with any child who does not already have one.

Family Spiritual Practice

SAY: Let's take a look at your Take-Home Pages for today *(Reproducibles 6F–6G)*. Ask your family to participate in this week's spiritual practice.

Supplemental Activities

Preschoolers – Build a Bush

Supplies: interlocking blocks in red, yellow, orange, brown, and green

SAY: The bush that God spoke from was on fire, but it was not burning up. Remember, our Faith Word is *awe*.

ASK: Would you be filled with awe if you saw a bush on fire, but not burning up?

• Have the children build a burning bush out of the interlocking blocks.

WONDER: Have you been asked to do something you didn't think you could do? Did you make excuses for not doing it?

Early Elementary – Burning Bush Candleholder

Supplies: clear plastic cups; gluesticks; red, yellow, and orange tissue paper; battery-operated tea light candles (one for each child)

• Place red, orange, and yellow tissue paper in the center of the table.

• Give each child a clear plastic cup and a gluestick.

• Encourage each child to tear the tissue paper into small pieces and glue the pieces to cover the outside of a clear plastic cup.

• Give each child a battery-operated tea light candle to place inside his or her cup.

Older Elementary – Curiosity Walk

WONDER: When is the last time you felt curious about something?

• Lead the children to take a curiosity walk with you around your church campus (either inside or out). Invite the children to walk quietly, only speaking if they see something they are curious about. They must say the words "I'm curious about . . ." to share their findings.

• Once you are done and back in your space, have a discussion about your findings.

ASK: What surprised you about what you saw on our curiosity walk?

ASK: What does curiosity have to do with our relationship with God?

• Let the children discuss, as your time permits.

Intergenerational Activity – Birthday Party

Supplies: cupcakes, trick birthday candles (if available), regular birthday candles, a large glass bowl or container, disposable plates and napkins, utility lighter, optional: juice and cups

Prepare Ahead: Find out if there are any youth or adults with birthdays this week (or coming soon).

- Invite youth and adults to attend a short birthday party!
- Talk with your class before the guests arrive.

SAY: I have some trick birthday candles! Let's use these and see what happens when (*person having birthday*) tries to blow them out!

- Invite an older-elementary kid to put a few trick candles in a cupcake and have the child use the utility lighter to light the candles.
- Sing, "Happy Birthday," and invite your guest to blow out the candles.
- The candles will continue to relight. Show everyone a trick. Place the large glass bowl or container over the cupcake and candles. The lack of oxygen will eventually make the candles go out.

SAY: Moses will see a fire that won't burn out in today's Bible story.

- Invite everyone to enjoy their cupcakes.

The people were in awe of the LORD, and they believed in the LORD and in his servant Moses. (Exodus 14:31b)

Moses and the Pharaoh – Exodus 5:1–13:9

Prepare to Wonder

Faith Word: Awe

Moses has been placed in a river and saved by the pharaoh's daughter, killed an Egyptian, and escaped only to find he was called by God to return to Egypt and set his people free. Moses tried to get God to send someone else to Egypt, and while that didn't work, God agreed to send Moses' brother Aaron with him.

So, Aaron and Moses took off to convince the pharaoh to let the Israelites go. The pharaoh did not want to let the Israelites go. He needed them to build his massive buildings. Instead, when Moses and Aaron requested the Israelites be released, the pharaoh doubled their workload. Now, the Israelites were unhappy with Moses.

Then came the plagues. Nine times, Moses would ask the pharaoh to let God's people go. Pharaoh said no nine times. Nine times, something terrible happened. The pharaoh finally agreed to let the people go, but only after the firstborn sons of the Egyptians were killed.

We tend to use *awe* as a word to describe something wonderfully good. If that is true, where is the awe and wonder in this story? Could it be that the awe is in the persistence of Moses asking and the pharaoh saying no? How many of us would have given up after the first five nos? Maybe the awe was in the powerful acts that God performed. Or maybe the awe was when God instructed the Israelites to remember God's mighty acts that resulted in the release of the Israelites.

Spiritual Practice for Adults

Sit comfortably and close your eyes. Think of a time when you were upset because your plans didn't turn out the way you wanted. After some reflection, you discovered God was at work in your life. What you wanted was not what you needed. Thank God for unexpected blessings that God sends your way.

Come Together

Come Together

Supplies: Class Pack, Celebrate Wonder Bible Storybook, Wonder Box, green cloth, battery-operated candle, toy bugs and critters

Prepare Ahead: Set up a Wonder Table (see p. 3) with a green cloth, battery-operated candle, and a Wonder Box (see p. 3). Display the Unit 2 Bible Verse Poster (Class Pack—pp. 12 & 13) and Faith Word Poster (Class Pack—p. 21). Place the toy bugs and critters inside the Wonder Box.

- Point to the Unit 2 Faith Word Poster, and invite the children to wonder about what the word awe means.

- Invite the kids to join you in a circle.

SAY: This month we are hearing stories about a man named Moses. Our story today tells us what happened when Moses met with the pharaoh.

- Take a few minutes to talk about last week's Bible story.

- We recommend reading a story from the *Celebrate Wonder Bible Storybook.* Allow an elementary kid to read, "Moses and the Pharaoh" (pp. 54–55), from the storybook.

PRAY: Dear God, thank you for caring for people who are in danger. Thank you that we can help people who are in need. Give us courage to ask for help when we need it and to show help when we can. Amen.

Moses and the Pharaoh – Preschool

Supplies: Reproducible Kids' Book, crayons or markers

- Give each preschooler a photocopy of "Moses and the Pharaoh" (Reproducible 7A), and invite them to color the picture following the directions.

- Invite elementary kids to help the preschoolers understand the directions.

Burning Bush – Younger Elementary

Supplies: Reproducible Kids' Book, crayons or markers

- Hand out a photocopy of "Find the Matching Pictures" (Reproducible 7B) to each kid.

SAY: Frogs and locusts are in today's Bible story. Each frog and locust on the page has a match. Find the matches and draw a line connecting them.

- Invite the kids to find the matching frogs and locusts on the page and draw lines connecting the matches.

ASK: Did you find the matches?

SAY: We will learn more about the frogs and locusts in our Bible story today

The Plagues Word Search – Older Elementary

Supplies: Reproducible Kids' Book, pencils

- Hand out a photocopy of "The Plagues Word Search" (Reproducible 7C) to each kid.

SAY: When God saved the Hebrew people from slavery in Egypt, there were bad things that happened in the land called *plagues*. There were ten plagues that came to Egypt. Use the word bank at the bottom of the page to find the ten plagues in the puzzle.

- Invite the kids to solve the puzzle.
- The kids may work together on the puzzle, if they wish.

ASK: Did you find all of the words in today's word search?

SAY: We will learn more about the plagues in our Bible story today.

Learn About Passover – All Ages

Supplies: Reproducible Kids' Book, bowl of saltwater, celery sticks, matzo crackers, cups of water, horseradish, two large apples, applesauce, chopped raisins, cinnamon (two teaspoons), hard-boiled eggs (sliced), lamb bone (from a butcher shop), large bowl, knife (adult use only), mixing spoon

Prepare Ahead: Before class, prepare the haroseth. Chop two large apples into fine slices. Place them in a bowl. Add applesauce, chopped raisins, and two teaspoons of cinnamon. Mix the items together using a spoon.

- Provide the other items described on "Learn About Passover" (Reproducible 7D).
- Divide the kids into groups. Hand out a photocopy of Reproducible 7D to each group.

SAY: The events from today's Bible story are remembered in the celebration of Passover. Passover happens in the spring. But let's have a special Passover snack today!

- Invite the groups to follow the directions on Reproducible 7D to host a Passover Seder.

- Instruct the groups to take turns reading the information on the sheet.

- When the groups have finished, discuss the experience.

ASK: What did you learn about Passover?

SAY: Today we're learning about Moses. Passover helps us remember what happened in the Book of Exodus.

Wonder Time

Interactive Bible Story

Supplies: Reproducible Kids' Book

Prepare Ahead: Photocopy the Take-Home Pages from the Reproducible Kids' Book, 7F–7G (pp. 83–84).

- "Moses and the Pharaoh" is written in short sections that are one to three sentences long. Invite several readers to take turns reading the story one section at a time.

- Read through the story.

Share a Story

Supplies: Celebrate Wonder DVD, TV, DVD player

- Invite the children to join you, sitting in a circle on the floor.

- Watch the Session 7 video (Celebrate Wonder DVD).

Wonder with Me

Supplies: Class Pack, Wonder Box, scissors

Prepare Ahead: Lay out the Unit 2 Wonder Story Mat (Class Pack—pp. 8 & 17). Cut out the three remaining Unit 2 Bible story figures (Class Pack—p. 19), if not done already.

- Place the Wonder Box on the Unit 2 Wonder Story Mat.

SAY: Awe is the Faith Word today.

- Show the children the Unit 2 Faith Word Poster (Class Pack—p. 21).

SAY: In this unit, we are using this definition of awe: an amazing feeling of wonder inspired by God.

- Point to the timeline on the Unit 2 Wonder Story Mat.

WONDER together:

- ❍ What amazing things have happened to Moses so far?
- ❍ Why didn't Moses and Aaron give up when the pharaoh kept saying no?
- ❍ What do you think is the most awesome event in today's Bible story?

- Place the Bible story figure of Moses with his staff on the Wonder Story Mat, in the space above the previous two Moses figures.
- Open the Wonder Box to reveal the toy critters.

WONDER: What do all these critters have to do with the Bible story?

Experience Wonder

Pharaoh Says No and Go

- Have the children line up across one side of the room.
- Stand on the opposite side of the room and guide the children.
- When the pharaoh (the teacher) says, "Go," the children advance until the pharaoh says, "No." This is similar to "Red Light, Green Light."
- Play several rounds.

SAY: In our Bible story, Pharaoh kept changing his mind. One minute he would say they could go, and then he would say no they can't.

WONDER: Why do you think Pharaoh kept changing his mind? How do you think the Israelites felt when Pharaoh kept changing his mind?

Examine the Bible Verse

SAY: Our Unit 2 Bible verse is Exodus 14:31b. Find it in your Bibles.

ASK: Is the Book of Exodus in the Old or New Testament? (Old) Where is Exodus located in the Old Testament? (second book) What is the chapter number? (14) What is the verse number? (31b)

- Gather the kids around the Unit 2 Bible Verse Poster (Class Pack—pp. 12 & 13). Read it together.

ASK: What is the reference for our verse? (Exodus 14:31b)

Peaceful Place

Supplies: Celebrate Wonder Bible Storybook, suggested book: "Let My People Go!" by Tilda Balsley, play dough, toy bugs and critters, matching cards, paper, crayons or markers

- Assist the children, as needed, as they interact with the items provided.

- Invite the children to draw a picture of what Pharaoh looked like when he said no.

Tip: All of the supplies/activities suggested for the Peaceful Place are optional.

Go in Peace

Spiritual Practice – Exploring Awe Through Gratitude

Supplies: Leader Guide—pp. 111, 112; index cards; crayons or markers

SAY: Spiritual practice is something we do to help us connect to God. Connecting to God is the most important reason to do spiritual practice. This week we have heard how hard it was for Moses and Aaron to convince the pharaoh to let the Israelites go. When he finally said yes, Moses, Aaron, and the Israelites were very grateful.

- Guide the children through this spiritual practice.

ASK: What has happened today that you are thankful for?

SAY: Draw a picture on an index card of what you are thankful for.

PRAY: Repeat after me: "Thank you, God, for the wonder-filled stories in the Bible. Amen."

- Bless the children before they leave. Touch each child as you say this blessing: "May you always be filled with awe and gratitude for God's wonderful world."

- Send home a photocopy of the Family Letter (Leader Guide—p. 112) and a photocopy of the Celebration Chart (Leader Guide—p. 111) with any child who does not already have one.

Family Spiritual Practice

SAY: Ask your family to participate in this week's spiritual practice.

- Show the kids where to find the Family Spiritual Practice on the Take-Home Pages (Reproducible 7F).

Supplemental Activities

Preschoolers – Sand Fun

Supplies: containers with sand, plastic covering, plastic bugs/critters

Prepare Ahead: Cover the surface with a plastic covering. Place the sand container on top of the plastic covering.

• Have the children play freely with the sand and critters in the container.

SAY: God sent many plagues to convince Pharaoh to let the Israelites go. Each time the pharaoh said no, God sent a plague worse than the one before.

WONDER: When do you refuse to give up? Why do you think the pharaoh wouldn't let the Israelites go?

Early Elementary – Persistence and Plagues

Supplies: paper, crayons or markers

SAY: Moses told Pharaoh to let God's people go. Pharaoh said no, but Moses was persistent.

ASK: Do you know what *persistent* means?

SAY: *Persistent* means to try and try again. *Persistent* means to never give up trying. Write about or draw a picture of a time when you were persistent.

• Give each child a sheet of paper and something to write or draw with.

• Encourage the children to write or draw about a time they were persistent.

Older Elementary – Gratitude Journaling

Supplies: paper, pens or pencils, coloring supplies

SAY: We come with our own experiences of awe as we remember what God has done for us. Take some time to think of how you see God, and give thanks to God today.

• Invite the children to write or draw as they reflect on the things they are grateful for. Both are important ways for them to express and reflect.

• When everyone has had time to write or create, allow the children to share their thoughts. Be sure to share your own as well.

WONDER: How might you take time to be in awe of God this week?

• Encourage the children to carry a heart of gratitude with them as they go through their week.

Intergenerational Activity – Build a Pyramid

Supplies: Reproducible Kids' Book; big building blocks, cardboard boxes, or something similar

Prepare Ahead: Make several photocopies of "Pyramid Building" (Reproducible 7E).

SAY: The Bible stories we've been learning about all happen in the land of Egypt.

ASK: What do you think of when you think about the land of Egypt?

- Have the kids, youth, and adults discuss the question. Someone may suggest the pyramids. If no one mentions it, try to get the group to come up with that answer using some hints.

SAY: We are going to work together to make our own pyramids.

- Divide the kids, youth, and adults into groups.

- Hand each group a copy of Reproducible 7E.

- Invite the groups to follow the directions on Reproducible 7E, including the discussion. Then bring the groups back together.

ASK: If God makes a promise, will God keep that promise?

- Have the groups work together to clean up from the activity.

The people were in awe of the LORD, and they believed in the LORD and in his servant Moses. (Exodus 14:31b)

Crossing the Sea –
Exodus 13:17–14:31

Prepare to Wonder

Faith Word: Awe

Pharaoh finally agreed to let the Israelites go. They quickly gathered what they could and left. Moses was now in charge of getting thousands of people out of Egypt. Whatever doubts Moses may have had, he was reminded daily that God was with him. God led the people with a column of clouds by day and a column of lightning by night. I can only imagine the awe the Israelites must have felt following God in the clouds and the lightning!

It didn't take long for the pharaoh to change his mind again. While the people were camped by the Reed Sea, Pharaoh's army caught up to them. The people were afraid and blamed Moses for leading them to the desert to die. They needed a lot of convincing that the God of Moses was with them.

Moses trusted God, and his faith did not waver. When God told him to point his rod towards the sea, Moses did not hesitate. The Reed Sea parted, the Israelites went through, and when Moses pointed his rod again, the sea came together. The Egyptians were stopped on the other side of the Reed Sea. The Israelites were in awe when they saw the mighty power of God.

The Bible story today is just the beginning of a long journey for the Israelites. They would continue to doubt God's presence, and God would continue to perform awe-inspiring acts.

Spiritual Practice for Adults

Sit comfortably and close your eyes. Imagine you are walking through the sea with the Israelites. What do you see? What do you hear? What do you feel? What action has God done in your life that was so awe-inspiring, you knew immediately it was God? Thank God for always being present with you.

Come Together

Come Together

Supplies: Class Pack, Celebrate Wonder Bible Storybook, Wonder Box, green cloth, battery-operated candle, spray bottle

Prepare Ahead: Set up a Wonder Table (see p. 3) with a green cloth, battery-operated candle, and a Wonder Box (see p. 3). Display the Unit 2 Bible Verse Poster (Class Pack—pp. 12 & 13) and Faith Word Poster (Class Pack—p. 21). Place the spray bottle inside the Wonder Box.

- Point to the Unit 2 Faith Word Poster, and invite the children to wonder about what the word *awe* means.

- Invite the kids to join you in a circle.

SAY: This month we are hearing stories about a man named Moses. Our story today tells us what happened when the Hebrews left Egypt.

- Take a few minutes to talk about last week's Bible story.

- We recommend reading a story from the *Celebrate Wonder Bible Storybook*. Allow an elementary kid to read, "Crossing the Sea" (pp. 56–57), from the storybook.

PRAY: Dear God, thank you for caring for people who are in danger. Thank you that when we are afraid, we can ask you for help. Amen.

Crossing the Sea – Preschool

Supplies: Reproducible Kids' Book, crayons or markers

Prepare Ahead: Photocopy "Crossing the Sea" (Reproducible 8A) for each child.

ASK: What's happening in the picture?

SAY: God made the water move, so the people could go across!

- Give each preschooler a copy of the reproducible page, and invite them to color the picture following the directions.

- Invite elementary kids to help the preschoolers, as needed.

Crossing the Sea – Younger Elementary

Supplies: Reproducible Kids' Book, white card stock, watercolor paints, brushes, cups of water, a few saltshakers, scissors, colored pencils, crayons, paper towels, pencils

Prepare Ahead: *Photocopy "Crossing the Sea" (Reproducible 8B) onto white card stock for each child. Make the watercolor painting supplies available.*

- Hand out a copy of Reproducible 8B to each kid.

- Have the kids color the circles on the page as they wish. The circles represent the Hebrew people crossing on dry land. The kids can also color the area around the circles using a brown crayon or colored pencil.

- Invite the kids to cut out the overall square on the page.

- Instruct the kids to put their names on the front or back of the page.

- Next, have the kids fold the top of the square down to the middle so that the circles on the page are partially hidden.

- Then have the kids fold the bottom of the square up to the middle so that the circles are completely hidden.

- Instruct the kids to keep the card stock folded so that the "people" crossing (the circles) remain hidden.

- Have the kids use blue watercolors to paint the card stock. Next, invite the kids to shake a little salt on the wet watercolors.

- Set the pictures aside to dry.

- After the pictures have dried, discuss how the picture relates to today's Bible story. Have the kids fold and unfold the artwork to imagine how the Reed Sea parted and the Hebrew people walked across dry land.

SAY: In today's Bible story, God made the waters of the Reed Sea part. A wind came and kept the waters parted. Then the Hebrew people walked across on dry land!

- Invite the kids to help clean up after the activity has concluded.

Missing Vowels – Older Elementary

Supplies: Reproducible Kids' Book, pencils

- Hand out a photocopy of "Missing Vowels" (Reproducible 8C) to each kid.

SAY: This month's Bible verse is from Exodus 14:31b. The verse is printed on the page, but the vowels are missing. Use the number of missing vowels at the bottom of the page to fill in the missing letters.

- Invite the kids to work together to determine the missing vowels from the Bible verse. If the kids get stuck, suggest that they look up the Bible verse from Exodus 14:31b.

- Invite the kids to share the Bible verse with the class.

Let My People Go – All Ages

Supplies: *white card stock, paper plate, blue marker, large craft stick, duct tape (white, if available), masking tape*

Prepare Ahead: *Make a Stop/Go sign using the paper plate. On one side of the paper plate, use a blue marker to make a lot of blue wavy lines. Then flip the plate over. On the other side, attach half of the craft stick to the paper plate using duct tape. White duct tape is even better, if available.*

- Mark a start line at one end of your classroom using masking tape. At the other end of the classroom, mark a finish line with masking tape.

- To play the game, invite all the kids to line up behind the start line. There are no teams; every player is on his or her own.

- Stand halfway between the start and finish line holding the Stop/Go sign you made.

SAY: In today's Bible story, the Hebrew people are going to leave Egypt. They will have to cross the Reed Sea. To do that, God will make a path straight through the sea. When I hold my sign with the blue waves showing, that means "Don't go." The sea is still an obstacle for you. But when I flip the sign around *(demonstrate),* you may walk to other side of the room. If the sign flips back to waves, you must stop!

- Play the game, flipping the sign back and forth. Emphasize that the kids should walk, not run.

- Play multiple times as the kids have interest.

Wonder Time

Interactive Bible Story

Supplies: *Reproducible Kids' Book*

Prepare Ahead: *Photocopy the Take-Home Pages from the Reproducible Kids' Book, 8F–8G (pp. 85–86).*

- "Crossing the Sea" is written in short sections that are one to three sentences long. Invite several readers to take turns reading the story one section at a time.

- Read through the story.

Share a Story

Supplies: *Celebrate Wonder DVD, TV, DVD player*

- Invite the children to join you, sitting in a circle on the floor.
- Watch the Session 8 video (Celebrate Wonder DVD).

Wonder with Me

Supplies: Class Pack, Wonder Box, scissors, tape

Prepare Ahead: Lay out the Unit 2 Wonder Story Mat (Class Pack—pp. 8 & 17). Cut out the remaining two Unit 2 Bible story figures (Class Pack—p. 19), if you have not done so already.

- Place the Wonder Box on the Unit 2 Wonder Story Mat.

SAY: *Awe is the Faith Word today.*

- Show the children the Unit 2 Faith Word Poster (Class Pack—p. 21).

SAY: *In this unit, we are using this definition of awe: an amazing feeling of wonder inspired by God.*

- Point to the timeline on the Wonder Story Mat.

WONDER together:

  ○ What do you think the Israelites felt going through the Reed Sea?

  ○ Where do you see God in this Bible story?

  ○ I wonder how God made the sea part. What do you think?

  ○ How did the Israelites feel when they made it safely through the sea?

- Place the Bible story figure of Moses parting the sea on the Wonder Story Mat, above the three other Moses figures.
- Open the Wonder Box to reveal the spray bottle, and mist the children with the water.

WONDER: *I wonder why there is a spray bottle in our Wonder Box. What does a spray bottle have to do with our story?*

Experience Wonder

Crossing the Sea – Make a Comic

Supplies: Reproducible Kids' Book, crayons, markers, colored pencils

Prepare Ahead: Make a photocopy of "Crossing the Sea" (Reproducible 8D) for each kid.

- Have older-elementary kids pair with younger kids to assist with reading as needed.

- Invite the kids to read the words in the comic panels.
- Invite the kids to draw the scenes as they are described in the comic panels.
- Have the kids color their comics.

SAY: God rescued the Hebrew people in today's story!

Examine the Bible Verse

SAY: Our Unit 2 Bible verse is Exodus 14:31b. Find it in your Bibles.

ASK: Is the Book of Exodus in the Old or New Testament? *(Old)* Where is Exodus located in the Old Testament? *(second book)* What is the chapter number? *(14)* What is the verse number? *(31b)*

- Gather the kids around the Unit 2 Bible Verse Poster (Class Pack—pp. 12 & 13) Read it together.

ASK: What is the reference for our verse? *(Exodus 14:31b)*

Peaceful Place

Supplies: Celebrate Wonder Bible Storybook, suggested book: "Being Thankful" by Mercer Mayer, water tray with plastic fish, sand tray, paper, crayons

- Assist the children, as needed, as they interact with the items provided.
- Invite the children draw a picture of what they imagine going through the sea looked like.

Tip: All of the supplies/activities suggested for the Peaceful Place are optional.

Go in Peace

Spiritual Practice – Exploring Awe Through Gratitude

Supplies: index cards, crayons or markers

SAY: Spiritual practice is something we do to help us connect to God. It doesn't have to be the same spiritual practice all the time, but it can be. There is no right or wrong way to do spiritual practice. Connecting to God is the most important reason to do a spiritual practice. The last few weeks, we have heard stories of Moses and the many awesome acts God performed to save the Israelites.

- Guide the children through this spiritual practice.

ASK: When do you feel thankful to God?

SAY: Draw a picture of something you are thankful for on an index card.

PRAY: Repeat after me: "God, help me always be thankful for you. Amen."

- Bless the children before they leave. Touch each child as you say this blessing: "May you always be filled with awe and gratitude for God's wonderful world."

Family Spiritual Practice

- Show the kids where to find the Family Spiritual Practice on the Take-Home Pages (Reproducible 8F).

Supplemental Activities

Preschoolers – Chalk Painting

Supplies: black or blue construction paper, colored chalk, spray bottle, water

- Have the children draw the Reed Sea on the construction paper with chalk.
- After the children have completed their pictures, lightly mist them with water and watch the colors change.

SAY: The Israelite people were afraid as Pharaoh's army got closer. They had nowhere to go because the sea was in front of them. God did not leave them alone. God made a way through the sea so they would be saved.

WONDER: What do you think the Israelites thought when they saw the sea part? What would you think if you saw a sea part in front of you? Would you trust God that you would make it across?

Early and Older Elementary – Ocean Bottles

Supplies: clear plastic bottles, funnel, large pitcher of water, vegetable or baby oil, blue food coloring, duct tape, optional: tiny plastic fish or shells

- Give child a clear plastic bottle.
- Help the child use the funnel to fill the bottle about half full of water, and then add several drops of blue food coloring.
- Then help the child fill the rest of the bottle with vegetable or olive oil, and tightly replace the cap.

Optional: Invite the child to add a few tiny fish or shells to his or her bottle.

- Place a strip of duct tape around the cap to make it extra secure.
- Encourage each child to explore the ocean bottle as you help other children create theirs.

Intergenerational Activity – Cookie Path

Supplies: large sugar cookies, white frosting, blue sprinkles, large bag of candy-coated chocolates, index cards, disposable plates and napkins, disposable knives, optional: cups and milk

Tip: Always check for food allergies before serving a snack.

- Invite youth and adults to join you for this activity, if you wish.

SAY: In today's Bible story, the Hebrew people are going to leave Egypt. They will have to cross the Reed Sea. To do that, God will make a path straight through the sea. Let's decorate cookies that remind us of today's story.

- Invite the kids to spread a layer of frosting on their cookies.

- Next, have them put a few candy-coated chocolates in the center of the cookie. The candy represents people crossing on dry land.

- Invite the kids to use an index card as they shake blue sprinkles on either side of the "people" (candy-coated chocolates). The index card keeps the sprinkles from covering the center of the cookie.

- Invite the kids to enjoy their cookies and help clean up when they are finished. (Optional: Pour cups of milk for the kids.)

The people were in awe of the LORD, and they believed in the LORD and in his servant Moses. (Exodus 14:31b)

Moses and Miriam Celebrate – Exodus 15:1-21

Prepare to Wonder

Faith Word: Awe

God acted in awesome ways to deliver the Israelites from slavery in Egypt. Moses was saved by the pharaoh's daughter and grew into adulthood, with all the privileges of the pharaoh's family. Amazingly, God called to Moses from a burning bush and sent him back to Egypt to free God's people. Eventually, God's powerful acts convinced the pharaoh to let the Israelites go. To ensure the people got out of Egypt safely, God performed another awe-inspiring act by parting the Reed Sea. The people believed God was with them, and it was time to celebrate!

Miriam, the sister of Moses, led the people in song and dance to celebrate their freedom. Miriam and her song, "Sing to the Lord," was a song of praise and a song of remembrance. God wants the people to remember the many ways God cares for God's people. The spiritual practice for this unit is exploring awe through gratitude. This Bible story is one of gratitude. Gratitude is not always shown in wild celebration. Remind the children that gratitude can also be expressed through quiet prayer and silent reflection.

Spiritual Practice for Adults

Find a comfortable place to sit and close your eyes. Imagine you have just walked through a sea that God parted for you. Imagine you are on the other side of the sea and no longer in slavery. For the first time in your life, you are free to worship the God of your ancestors. How would you choose to celebrate? How would you remember the amazing acts God performed for you? Praise God through song or prayer. Praise God for all the amazing ways God has delivered you safely from times of trouble.

Come Together

Come Together

Supplies: Class Pack, Celebrate Wonder Bible Storybook, Wonder Box, green cloth, battery-operated candle, party hat

Prepare Ahead: Set up a Wonder Table (see p. 3) with a green cloth, battery-operated candle, and a Wonder Box (see p. 3). Display the Unit 2 Bible Verse Poster (Class Pack—pp. 12 & 13) and Faith Word Poster (Class Pack—p. 21). Place the party hat inside the Wonder Box.

- Point to the Unit 2 Faith Word Poster, and invite the children to wonder about what the word *awe* means.

- Invite the kids to join you in a circle.

SAY: Last week we heard how the Hebrew people crossed the Reed Sea on dry land. Our story today tells us about how Moses and Miriam celebrated.

- Read today's story from the *Celebrate Wonder Bible Storybook*. Allow an elementary kid to read, "Miriam and Moses Celebrate" (pp. 58–59), from the storybook to the preschoolers.

- Invite the kids to share their favorite part of the story.

PRAY: Dear God, thank you for saving the Hebrew people. Thank you that you help us when we are in need too. Amen.

Moses and Miriam Celebrate – Preschool

Supplies: Reproducible Kids' Book, crayons or markers

- Give each preschooler a photocopy of "Moses and Miriam Celebrate" (Reproducible 9A).

SAY: God saved the Hebrew people! Moses and Miriam celebrated. Color Miriam holding a tambourine. Then color Moses. Color the rest of the picture.

- Invite the kids to color the page.

What's Wrong? – Younger Elementary

Supplies: Reproducible Kids' Book, crayons or colored pencils

Prepare Ahead: Before class, make a photocopy of "What's Wrong?" (Reproducible 9B) for each child.

- Hand out a copy of Reproducible 9B to each kid.

SAY: Miriam and Moses have reasons to celebrate. But this picture isn't quite right! Circle ten items that are wrong. Then color the page.

- Invite the kids to circle the items that are wrong.
- Have the kids color the page.

SAY: We will hear more about how Moses, Miriam, and the Hebrew people celebrated after they crossed the Reed Sea on dry land.

Which Sea? – Older Elementary

Supplies: *Reproducible Kids' Book, Bibles (NRSV and CEB), pencils*

Prepare Ahead: *Before class, make a photocopy of "Which Sea?" (Reproducible 9C) for each child.*

- Hand out a copy of Reproducible 9C to each kid.
- Invite the kids to solve the coded message using the directions on the page.
- Assist the kids if they get stuck or suggest they work together, if needed.
- Then have the kids use Bibles to find Exodus 13:18 in a *New Revised Standard Bible* and a *Common English Bible.*

ASK: What sea did the Hebrew people cross?

SAY: In some Bibles, it reads "Red Sea." In other Bibles, it reads "Reed Sea." These are two different seas, and we are not sure which sea the Hebrews crossed! That's okay. It's important to remember that God rescued the Hebrew people from danger.

Moses and Miriam Puppets – All Ages

Supplies: *Reproducible Kids' Book, white card stock, pencils, scissors, gluesticks, large craft sticks, tape, paper clips*

Prepare Ahead: *Use "Moses and Miriam Puppet Patterns" (Reproducible 9D) to create sets of shape templates, one set for each child. Photocopy the page onto card stock. Cut out the shapes and keep each set of fours shapes together with a paper clip.*

SAY: Let's make puppets of Moses and Miriam.

- To make the puppets, have the children trace around the shape templates on different colors of construction paper.
- Have them cut out the shapes, arrange them, and glue them using "Moses and Miriam Puppet Instructions" (Reproducible 9E) as a guide.

- Older kids should be able to make their own puppets and help preschool kids with tracing or cutting.
- Instruct the kids to put a large craft stick on the back of each of their puppets, securing the sticks with tape.
- Have the kids put their names on the back of their puppets. Keep the puppets in the classroom to use again in future sessions.

SAY: We will make our puppets dance and celebrate later on.

Wonder Time

Interactive Bible Story

Supplies: *Reproducible Kids' Book*

Prepare Ahead: *Photocopy the Take-Home Pages from the Reproducible Kids' Book, 9F–9G (pp. 87–88).*

- "Miriam and Moses Celebrate" is written in short sections that are one to three sentences long. Invite several readers to take turns reading the story one section at a time.
- Read through the story.

Share a Story

Supplies: *Celebrate Wonder DVD, TV, DVD player*

- Invite the children to join you, sitting in a circle on the floor.
- Watch the Session 9 video (Celebrate Wonder DVD).

Wonder with Me

Supplies: *Class Pack, Wonder Box, scissors, tape*

Prepare Ahead: *Lay out the Unit 2 Wonder Story Mat (Class Pack—pp. 8 & 17). Cut out the final figure from the Unit 2 Bible story figures (Class Pack—p. 19), if you did not already do so.*

- Place the Wonder Box on the Unit 2 Wonder Story Mat.

SAY: *Awe is the Faith Word today.*

- Show the children the Unit 2 Faith Word Poster (Class Pack—p. 21).

SAY: *Awe is an amazing feeling of wonder inspired by God.*

- Point to the timeline on the Wonder Story Mat.

WONDER together:

- ○ What was the most amazing act God performed?

- ○ How do you like to celebrate?

- ○ How do you like to thank God?

- Place the final Unit 2 Bible story figure of Moses dancing at the top of the Unit 2 Wonder Story Mat timeline.

- Open the Wonder Box to reveal the party hat.

WONDER: Why is there a party hat in the Wonder Box?

Experience Wonder

Celebration Time!

Supplies: Moses and Miriam puppets made earlier, CD of praise music, CD player or another way to play the music for your class

- Have the kids use the Moses and Miriam puppets made earlier. If you did not make the puppets earlier, you may choose to do so now (see p. 73).

- Have the kids take their puppets in each hand.

- Play music using the CD player or another method.

- As the music plays, invite the kids to bounce their puppets around to make them "dance" to the music.

SAY: God rescued the Hebrew people from danger!

Examine the Bible Verse

SAY: Our Unit 2 Bible verse is Exodus 14:31b. Find it in your Bibles.

ASK: Is the Book of Exodus in the Old or New Testament? *(Old)* Where is Exodus located in the Old Testament? *(second book)* What is the chapter number? *(14)* What is the verse number? *(31b)*

- Gather the kids around the Unit 2 Bible Verse Poster (Class Pack—pp. 12 & 13). Read it together.

ASK: What is the reference for our verse? *(Exodus 14:31b)*

Peaceful Place

Supplies: Celebrate Wonder Bible Storybook, suggested book: "The Birthday Book" by Todd Parr, play dough, birthday card-making supplies, paper, crayons or markers

- Assist the children, as needed, as they interact with the items provided.

- Have the children each make a birthday card for a friend.

- Invite the children to draw a picture of them praising God.

Tip: All of the supplies/activities suggested for the Peaceful Place are optional.

Go in Peace

Spiritual Practice – Exploring Awe Through Gratitude

Supplies: Leader Guide—pp. 111, 112; index cards; crayons or markers

SAY: A spiritual practice is something we do to help us connect to God. Sometimes we sing loudly or softly, sometimes we pray, sometimes we sit quietly and close our eyes. Connecting to God is the most important reason to do spiritual practice. We have spent several weeks exploring awe through gratitude.

- Guide the children through this spiritual practice.

ASK: When do you feel thankful to God?

SAY: Draw a picture of something you are thankful for on an index card.

PRAY: Repeat after me: "God, I am happy to praise and thank you! Amen."

- Bless the children before they leave. Touch each child as you say this blessing: "May you always be filled with awe and gratitude for God's wonderful world."

- Send home a photocopy of the Family Letter (Leader Guide—p. 112) and a photocopy of the Celebration Chart (Leader Guide—p. 111) with any child who does not already have one.

Family Spiritual Practice

- Show the kids where to find the Family Spiritual Practice on the Take-Home Pages (Reproducible 9F).

Supplemental Activities

Preschoolers – Tambourine

Supplies: stapler, sturdy paper plates, plastic beads, optional: decorative tape

- Give each child a paper plate.

- Invite each child to grab a handful of beads and place them in the center of a plate.

- Help each child staple a second paper plate over the plate holding the beads. The staples will have to go all the way around the paper plate to keep from losing beads.

SAY: Miriam and Moses led the Israelites in a song of praise and celebration when they were finally free. Miriam used a tambourine to add music to her song of praise.

- Invite the kids to shake their tambourines and celebrate!

WONDER: What musical instrument do you like? Miriam sang, "Praise the Lord!" What song do you like to sing when you praise God?

Tip: If the plates are white, let the children use crayons or markers to decorate the plates. Decorative tape is an option to decorate the edges.

Early Elementary – Gratitude Activity

Supplies: paper, pens or pencils, coloring supplies

SAY: We come with our own experiences of awe as we remember what God has done for us. Take some time to think of how you see God, and give thanks to God today.

- Invite the children to write or draw as they reflect. Both are important ways for them to express and reflect.

- When everyone has had time to write or create, allow the children to share their thoughts. Be sure to share your own as well.

WONDER: How might you take time to be in awe of God this week?

- Encourage the children to carry a heart of gratitude with them as they go through their week.

Older Elementary – Upcycled Praise Art

Supplies: art boards or cardboard squares, Tacky glue, cereal or other recycled food boxes that are colorful, bottle caps, other interesting recycled items, markers

Prepare Ahead: Gather recycled food boxes (clean) that are colorful in order for the children to make upcycled art

- In this activity, the children will be creating upcycled art to share the memory verse. The children will be given recycled supplies, simple art supplies, scissors, Tacky glue, and an art board/cardboard surface to create their own memory verse art.

- Write the memory verse somewhere easy for the children to read and copy: The people were in awe of the LORD, and they believed in the LORD and in his servant Moses. (Exodus 14:31b)

- Invite the children to write the memory verse on their art surface.

- Next, show them how they can cut different shapes out of the recycled cardboard and layer it onto the art surface to create their own upcycled art design. This is a fun and personal way to make a memory verse meaningful.

Intergenerational Activity – Freeze Dance

Supplies: CD of praise music, CD player or another way to play the music for your class

- Invite youth and adults to join you for this activity.

- Invite the participants to find a space in the room and to spread out.

- Play music from the CD or by another means.

- While the music plays, have the participants dance.

- Pause the music periodically. When the music stops, the participants should call out one thing they are thankful for. Participants do not need to take turns. Instead, encourage them to voice their thanksgiving all at once.

- Continue the activity, as time allows.

SAY: In today's session, we will hear how the Hebrew people celebrated and thanked God with song and dance!

The LORD your God is with you wherever you go. (Joshua 1:9b)

In the Wilderness – Exodus 15:22–17:7

Prepare to Wonder

Faith Word: TRUST

The Israelites were free and out of Egypt, but they were a long way from the land God promised. Instead, they found themselves in the wilderness. The soil was sandy, there was little vegetation, and water was scarce. Soon, the people were complaining. They began to doubt Moses and God.

The lack of food and water was real, but God was with them. God provided food by sending quail in the evening and manna in the morning. God cautioned the people to only take what food they needed for their family for that day and no more. Some people did not trust God and took more than they needed to save for later. When they went to eat the extra, they found it wormy and rancid.

Be sensitive to children who are food insecure. Humans have a tendency to believe in scarcity instead of God's provision, just like the Israelites in today's story. This has led some in our communities to keep more than they need, instead of ensuring everyone has what they need.

The spiritual practice for this unit is exploring trust through waiting. We are defining trust as believing God's love is always with you. The Israelites didn't know it, but they had many years and obstacles to overcome before they would arrive at the land God promised. They would have plenty of time to practice their waiting skills and learn to trust. Even when they doubted and complained, God was with them.

Spiritual Practice for Adults

This week locate a finger labyrinth. As you enter the labyrinth with your finger, remember the many times you have trusted God to provide for you. Is it easy to always to trust God? As you use your finger to come out of the labyrinth, pray that you will always trust that what God provides is what you need.

Tip: For more information on labyrinths, go to: http://www.lessons4living.com/labyrinth.htm.

Come Together

Come Together

Supplies: Class Pack, Celebrate Wonder Bible Storybook, Wonder Box, green cloth, battery-operated candle, empty travel bag

Prepare Ahead: Set up a Wonder Table (see p. 3) with a green cloth, battery-operated candle, and a Wonder Box (see p. 3). Display the Unit 3 Bible Verse Poster (Class Pack—pp. 9 & 16) and Faith Word Poster (Class Pack—p. 22). Place the empty travel bag inside the Wonder Box.

- Point to the Unit 3 Faith Word Poster, and invite the children to wonder about what the word *trust* means.

- Invite the kids to join you in a circle.

SAY: Last month we heard about Moses and how the Hebrew people were rescued from danger in Egypt. This month we will hear what happened next.

- Read today's story from the *Celebrate Wonder Bible Storybook*. You can allow an elementary kid to read, "In the Wilderness" (pp. 60–61), from the storybook to the preschoolers.

- Invite the kids to share their favorite part of the story.

PRAY: Dear God, thank you for showing us who you are. We love you and know that you love us! Amen.

In the Wilderness – Preschool

Supplies: Reproducible Kids' Book, crayons or markers

Prepare Ahead: Before class, photocopy Reproducible 10A for each preschooler.

- Give each preschooler a copy of "In the Wilderness" (Reproducible 10A).

SAY: God provided quail for the Hebrews to eat. What letter does quail start with? Find the letter and color it.

ASK: What letter did you find on the page? *(Q)*

- Invite the kids to color the quail and the rest of the page.

Wandering Maze – Younger Elementary

Supplies: Reproducible Kids' Book, crayons or colored pencils

Prepare Ahead: Before class, photocopy Reproducible 10B for each child.

- Hand out a copy of "Wandering Maze" (Reproducible 10B) to each child.

- Invite the kids to look over the maze from Reproducible 10B.

SAY: Moses and the Hebrew people wandered in the desert for a very long time. But what would they eat? God provided quail and manna for them to eat. Help Moses and the people find the food God provided for them.

- Instruct the kids to solve the maze.

- Invite the kids to work together, if needed.

- Invite the kids to color the page using colored pencils or crayons.

Silly Story – Older Elementary

Supplies: CEB Bibles, Reproducible Kids' Book, pencils

Prepare Ahead: Before class, photocopy Reproducible 10C for each child.

- Hand out a copy of "Silly Story" (Reproducible 10C) to each child.

- Invite older-elementary kids to fill in the blanks from Reproducible 10C, using the word prompt underneath each blank line.

- Have the kids share their silly versions of the Bible story for today.

- Have the kids look up the Bible passage from Exodus 16:1-31 in the *Common English Bible* to see how the story should be read.

ASK: What did you learn from the real version of today's Bible story?

Make "Stone" Tablets – All Ages

Supplies: Bibles, Reproducible Kids' Book; self-hardening clay; rolling pins; plastic knives, toothpicks, or other tools; wax paper; tape, index cards; pen or pencils; card stock; scissors; paper clips

Prepare Ahead: Use "Moses and Miriam Puppet Patterns" (Reproducible 9D) to create sets of shape templates, one set for each child. Photocopy the page onto card stock. Cut out the shapes and keep each set together with a paper clip.

- Hand out a few photocopies of "Make 'Stone' Tablets" (Reproducible 10D) to the kids.

- Spread out sheets of wax paper on the table and use tape to keep the sheets from rolling up.

- Give each kid a lump of self-hardening clay. Invite the kids to roll the clay out flat using a rolling pin.

- Invite the kids to work together following the directions from Reproducible 10D to make two stone tablets.

- Have the kids write the words *Love God* on one tablet and *Love Others* on the other tablet using a knife, toothpick, or other tool. Younger kids may need some help. Ask older-elementary kids to help, as needed.

- The clay will air-dry. Plan to set the clay aside in your classroom until next Sunday. Have each kid put their name on an index card (help preschoolers as needed). Place the kids' tablets on their index card somewhere in the classroom.

- Read Matthew 22:37-40.

SAY: God gave Moses rules for the people to follow. There were many rules! But Jesus said there were only two rules to remember.

Wonder Time

Interactive Bible Story

Supplies: Reproducible Kids' Book

Prepare Ahead: Photocopy the Take-Home Pages from the Reproducible Kids' Book, 10F–10G (pages 89–90).

- "In the Wilderness" is written in short sections that are one to three sentences long. Invite several readers to take turns reading the story one section at a time.

- Read through the story.

Share a Story

Supplies: Celebrate Wonder DVD, TV, DVD player

- Invite the children to join you, sitting in a circle on the floor.

- Watch the Session 10 video (Celebrate Wonder DVD).

Wonder with Me

Supplies: Class Pack, Wonder Box, scissors

Prepare Ahead: Lay out the Unit 3 Wonder Story Mat (Class Pack—pp. 11 & 14). Cut out the four Unit 3 Bible story figures (Class Pack—p. 3).

- Place the Wonder Box on the Unit 3 Wonder Story Mat.

SAY: Today's Faith Word is *trust*.

- Show the children the Unit 3 Faith Word Poster (Class Pack—p. 22).

SAY: In this unit, we define *trust* as believing God's love is always with you.

WONDER together:

○ Do you think the Israelites trusted God in this Bible story?

○ Do you think Moses trusted God in this Bible story?

○ Can you choose which figure goes with the Bible story?

• Have a child place the figure of people gathering manna and quail onto the Unit 3 Wonder Story Mat.

• Open the Wonder Box to reveal the empty travel bag.

WONDER: Do you know what this is? What does it have to do with our Bible story?

Experience Wonder

Manna Snack

Supplies: plates, napkins, small marshmallows, thin crackers, small squares of bread

• Give each child a plate with marshmallows, crackers, and small squares of bread.

SAY: No one really knows what the manna was that God sent. The word *manna* means, "What is it?" Some people think it was like marshmallows. Others think it may have been like a cracker. Still others think it was like bread.

• Let the children eat the food on their plates.

WONDER: What do you think manna was like?

Examine the Bible Verse

SAY: Our Unit 3 Bible verse is Joshua 1:9b. Find it in your Bibles.

ASK: Is the Book of Joshua in the Old or New Testament? *(Old)*

ASK: Where is Joshua located in the Old Testament? *(sixth book)* What is the chapter number? *(1)* What is the verse number? *(9b)*

• Gather the kids around the Unit 3 Bible Verse Poster (Class Pack—pp. 9 & 16). Read it together.

ASK: What is the reference for our verse? *(Joshua 1:9b)*

Peaceful Place

Supplies: Leader Guide—p. 115, Celebrate Wonder Bible Storybook, suggested book: "It Will Be Okay: Trusting God Through Fear and Change" by Lysa TerKeurst, sand tray, finger labyrinth, crayons

Prepare Ahead: Photocopy the Unit 3 Faith Word coloring sheet (Leader Guide—p. 115) for each child. Make extra copies of the Unit 3 Faith Word coloring sheet to leave in the Peaceful Place this month.

- Help the children, as needed, as they interact with the items provided.
- Have each child color the Faith Word coloring sheet.

Tip: All of the supplies/activities suggested for the Peaceful Place are optional.

Go in Peace

Spiritual Practice – Exploring Trust Through Waiting

Supplies: Leader Guide—pp. 111, 112; Reproducible Kids' Book

Prepare Ahead: Photocopy "Finger Labyrinth" (Reproducible 10E) for each child.

SAY: A spiritual practice is something we do to help us connect to God. Connecting to God is the most important reason to do a spiritual practice, not how you do it.

- Tell the children the labyrinth has been used for thousands of years to help people pray. Show the children how to trace their finger from the outside into the middle of the labyrinth and back out again.
- Guide the children through this spiritual practice.

SAY: Repeat after me as you guide your finger into the middle of the labyrinth: "God, help me trust you always." As you move your finger out of the labyrinth, say, "I will always trust you. Amen."

- Bless the children before they leave. Touch each child as you say this blessing: "May you be blessed by trusting God."
- Send home a photocopy of the Family Letter (Leader Guide—p. 112) and a photocopy of the Celebration Chart (Leader Guide—p.111) with any child who does not already have one.

Family Spiritual Practice

- Show the kids where to find the Family Spiritual Practice on the Take-Home Pages (Reproducible 10F).

Supplemental Activities

Preschoolers – Sand Picture

Supplies: plastic table covering, trays, construction paper, resealable snack bags, play sand, bowl, crayons or markers, scissors, glue

Prepare Ahead: Cover the table. Fill the resealable snack bags half full of sand. Snip a small cut in one corner of the bag. Store upside down in a bowl until ready to give to the children.

SAY: The Israelites were in the wilderness. The wilderness was like a desert. It had lots of sand and not much water or plants. They were hungry and started complaining to Moses. God said they would have enough food for one day at a time.

- Have the children draw a picture of the Israelites collecting the manna and quail.

- Have the children put glue on the paper where they want sand. Show them how to use the snipped corner of the bag to sprinkle sand over the glue. Let the glue dry.

WONDER: Have you ever been to a place with a lot of sand? What kinds of food might you find growing in a sandy place? What kinds of animals might you see?

Early Elementary – Forty Years

Supplies: paper, crayons or markers

SAY: The Israelites spent forty years in the desert traveling to the Promised Land. If you left on a trip today, how old would you be when you arrived? If you were like the Israelites, you'd be your age, plus forty years! How old is that?

- Encourage the children to draw self-portraits of themselves when they are forty years older.

Older Elementary – Trust Hula-Hoop Challenge

Supplies: Hula-Hoops (one per group)

- In this active game, you will lead the children through a Hula-Hoop pass game. Instruct them to work together to accomplish the challenges. They cannot break free of holding hands or allow the Hula-Hoop to drop to the floor.

  ○ Challenge 1: Gather the children in a circle, holding hands. In this challenge, the children must move the Hula-Hoop from the beginning to the end of the circle while holding hands and not dropping the group Hula-Hoop. To make it extra challenging, time the groups!

  ○ Challenge 2: The children will work together to carry the Hula-Hoop from point A to point B, without using their hands. This can look like a relay between groups too.

  ○ Challenge 3: The children only use their feet to move the Hula-Hoop from point A to point B.

WONDER: Why was trust important in order to complete today's challenges?

Intergenerational Activity – What I Like

Supplies: pictures of food from the internet, markerboard or large sheet of paper, markers

Prepare Ahead: *Find pictures of different kinds of food from the internet. Provide a wide variety of vegetables, proteins, desserts, and so forth. You may simply store the photos on your smartphone or print them out, if more convenient.*

SAY: We all need to eat food to stay healthy and to stay alive. But we all don't like the same foods. Let's look at some pictures of different foods. If you like the food, give me a thumbs-up. If you don't like the food, give me a thumbs-down.

- Invite the group to look at the pictures and give a thumbs-up or thumbs-down for each food they see. Keep score on the markerboard or on a large sheet of paper.

- Encourage the group not to make vocal comments about the food during this part of the activity. After the group has looked at all the food pictures, the group will discuss their choices.

- After looking at all the pictures of food, invite the group to look at the scores on the markerboard or large sheet of paper.

- Have the group discuss the foods they looked at together. Listen to hear from the older participants in the group. Were there foods they didn't like as kids that they like or love now? Are there any foods they've never liked?

SAY: Our taste in food changes over time. Just because you don't like something now doesn't mean you won't like it later in life! We learned Hebrew people complained about the wilderness, but God provided food for them to keep them healthy and alive.

The LORD your God is with you wherever you go. (Joshua 1:9b)

The Ten Commandments – Exodus 19:1–20:21

Prepare to Wonder

Faith Word: TRUST

Three months after leaving Egypt, Moses and the Israelites reached the Sinai desert and camped at the foot of Mt. Sinai. The Israelites were learning to trust that God would be with them and care for them. They had already experienced God moving them safely out of Egypt and God providing for them when they were hungry. However, the Israelites had a long way to go before arriving in the land God promised.

Trust is important for people who live in community. You must be able to trust your neighbor not to harm you. Trust in others does not always happen quickly. Sometimes it takes years to establish a trusting community. God knew the Israelites needed help to establish trust in their newly forming community. God called Moses to the top of Mt. Sinai to give him the set of rules the people were to live by.

We commonly refer to these rules as the Ten Commandments. The Ten Commandments were a set of rules God knew the Israelites needed to live in community. The first four commandments address the relationship between God and the Israelites. The next six commandments address the relationship between the people. Treating everyone with love and respect would ensure there would be trust between the people, and result in a loving and trusting community.

Spiritual Practice for Adults

Take some time to assess how well you are following the rules God gave Moses. Concentrate on the first four commandments and your relationship with God. How are you doing with number four? Remember the Sabbath day and treat it as holy. That is hard to do in today's nonstop world. This week commit to honor the Sabbath. What will get in the way of you resting and practicing Sabbath? Get the obstructions out of the way and spend time growing closer to God.

Come Together

Come Together

Supplies: Class Pack, Celebrate Wonder Bible Storybook, Wonder Box, green cloth, battery-operated candle, tic-tac-toe game

Prepare Ahead: Set up a Wonder Table (see p. 3) with a green cloth, battery-operated candle, and a Wonder Box (see p. 3). Display the Unit 3 Bible Verse Poster (Class Pack—pp. 9 & 16) and Faith Word Poster (Class Pack—p. 22). Place the tic-tac-toe game inside the Wonder Box.

- Point to the Unit 3 Faith Word Poster, and invite the children to wonder about what the word *trust* means.

- Invite the kids to join you in a circle.

SAY: Last month we heard about Moses and how the Hebrew people were rescued from danger in Egypt. This month we are learning what happened next.

- Read today's story from the *Celebrate Wonder Bible Storybook*. You can allow an elementary kid to read, "The Ten Commandments" (pp. 62–63), from the storybook to the preschoolers.

- Invite the kids to share their favorite part of the story.

PRAY: Dear God, thank you for giving us rules to live by. Your rules help us learn and grow. Amen.

The Ten Commandments – Preschool

Supplies: Reproducible Kids' Book, crayons or markers

Prepare Ahead: Before class, photocopy Reproducible 11A for each preschooler.

- Give each preschooler a copy of "The Ten Commandments" (Reproducible 11A).

SAY: When God wanted to give Moses the rules to live by, God told Moses to climb up the mountain.

ASK: Where do you feel close to God?

- Share a place you feel close to God with the preschoolers.

Stone Tablet – Younger Elementary

Supplies: Reproducible Kids' Book, colored pencils or markers, scissors

Prepare Ahead: Before class, photocopy Reproducible 11B for each child.

- Hand out a copy of "Stone Tablet" (Reproducible 11B) to each child.

- Direct the kids to look over the page from Reproducible 11B.

SAY: Cut on the two solid lines. Then fold the paper along the dotted line, covering the tablet and words. Hold the folded sheet up to a window. Use a pencil or marker to trace over the tablet and words.

- Instruct the kids to follow the directions, helping them as needed.

SAY: In today's Bible story, we will hear how God gave Moses and the Hebrew people commandments, or rules, to follow. We will hear how those rules help us love God and love others.

Commandment Matching – Older Elementary

Supplies: CEB Bibles, Reproducible Kids' Book, pencils

Prepare Ahead: Photocopy Reproducible 11C for each child.

- Hand out a copy of "Commandment Matching" (Reproducible 11C) to each kid.

SAY: Use Exodus 20 from a *Common English Bible* to match the commandments *(paraphrased)* to the correct number on the right.

- Have the kids follow the directions on the page, as needed.

ASK: What is the correct order for the Ten Commandments?

Ark of the Covenant – All Ages

Supplies: Reproducible Kids' Book, thin cardboard (from cereal boxes or something similar), tape, drinking straws, gluesticks

Prepare Ahead: Photocopy Reproducible 11D for each child.

- Hand out the copies of "Make the Ark of the Covenant" (Reproducible 11D) to the class, along with the supplies you gathered.

- Hand out the clay tablets your class may have made during last week's session. If you did not make clay tablets last week, consider making the tablets now (see p. 81).

- Invite the kids to follow the pictures and instructions from Reproducible 11D to make an ark of the covenant. Preschoolers and young-elementary kids will likely need help. Assist them, and invite older-elementary kids to assist them, as needed.

- Make sure the kids understand the clay tablets made earlier should fit inside their arks.

SAY: In today's Bible story, we heard how God gave Moses and the Hebrew people rules to live by. These rules, or commandments, were carved onto stone tablets.

- Place one set of clay tablets inside an ark made by the kids.

SAY: Later, we will hear how God instructed the Hebrew people to make a special box called the ark of the covenant. The box was very beautiful and covered with gold.

- If the kids in your class made facing angels for the lid of their arks, direct their attention to these angels now.

SAY: God instructed the Hebrew people to make angels facing each other for the lid of the ark. The ark of the covenant helped the people remember how special God's rules for living were.

- Set the arks aside in your classroom. If the kids in your class made an index card with their name on it last week, use these cards again to help remember which arks and which tablets belong to the kids. Plan to send the project home at the end of the month.

Wonder Time

Interactive Bible Story

Supplies: *Reproducible Kids' Book*

Prepare Ahead: *Photocopy the Take-Home Pages from the Reproducible Kids' Book, 11F–11G (pp. 91–92).*

- "The Ten Commandments" is written in short sections that are one to three sentences long. Invite several readers to take turns reading the story one section at a time.
- Read through the story.

Share a Story

Supplies: *Celebrate Wonder DVD, TV, DVD player*

- Invite the children to join you, sitting in a circle on the floor.
- Watch the Session 11 video (Celebrate Wonder DVD).

Wonder with Me

Supplies: *Class Pack, Wonder Box, scissors, tape*

Prepare Ahead: *Lay out the Unit 3 Wonder Story Mat (Class Pack—pp. 11 & 14). Cut out the three remaining Bible story figures (Class Pack—p. 3), if not done already.*

- Place the Wonder Box on the Unit 3 Wonder Story Mat.

SAY: Today's Faith Word is *trust*.

- Show the children the Unit 3 Faith Word Poster (Class Pack—p. 22).

SAY: In this unit, we define *trust* as believing God's love is always with you.

WONDER together:

 ○ Why do you think rules are important?

 ○ Why did God want the Israelites to follow the Ten Commandments?

 ○ Can you choose which figure goes with the Bible story?

- Have a child place the mountain (representing Mt. Sinai) onto the Unit 3 Wonder Story Mat.

- Open the Wonder Box to reveal the tic-tac-toe game.

WONDER: Why would we have a tic-tac-toe game in the Wonder Box?

Experience Wonder

Bonus Coloring Page

Supplies: Reproducible Kids' Book, crayons or markers

Prepare Ahead: Photocopy "Bonus Coloring Page" (Reproducible 11E) for each kid. Use the page as a bonus coloring page when the kids complete other activities.

- Invite the kids to work on the page, as time allows.

SAY: Moses went to the top of the mountain to meet with God. God gave Moses commandments *(or laws)* for the Hebrew people to follow. Color Moses.

ASK: Why do you think God gave the people rules to follow?

- Invite the kids to think about how God's rules helped the people live happy and healthy lives.

Examine the Bible Verse

SAY: Our Unit 3 Bible verse is Joshua 1:9b. Find it in your Bibles.

ASK: Is the Book of Joshua in the Old or New Testament? *(Old)*

ASK: Where is Joshua located in the Old Testament? *(sixth book)* What is the chapter number? *(1)* What is the verse number? *(9b)*

- Gather the kids around the Unit 3 Bible Verse Poster (Class Pack—pp. 9 & 16). Read it together.

ASK: What is the reference for our verse? *(Joshua 1:9b)*

Peaceful Place

Supplies: Celebrate Wonder Bible Storybook, suggested book: "But Why Can't I?" by Sue Graves, play dough, soft blocks, crayons or markers, paper

- Assist the children, as needed, as they interact with the items provided.

- Let the children build Mt. Sinai with the blocks or the play dough.

- Invite the children to draw someone they love, because the Ten Commandments help us love one another well.

Tip: All of the supplies/activities suggested for the Peaceful Place are optional.

Go in Peace

Spiritual Practice – Exploring Trust Through Waiting

Supplies: markerboard and erasable marker or posterboard and marker

SAY: A spiritual practice is something we do to help us connect to God. It doesn't have to be the same spiritual practice all the time, but it can be. There is no right or wrong way to do spiritual practice. Connecting to God is the most important reason for spiritual practices. Ten is an important number in the Bible story today. Let's come up with ten people we can trust to help us keep rules and stay safe.

- Guide the children through this spiritual practice.

- Have the children name someone, and write down the people the children name.

PRAY: Now let's pray for each of those people who help us stay safe. I will say the person's name, and you will say, "Thank you, God."

- Bless the children before they leave. Touch each child as you say this blessing: "May you be blessed by trusting God."

- Send home a photocopy of the Family Letter (Leader Guide—p. 112) and a photocopy of the Celebration Chart (Leader Guide—p. 111) with any child who does not already have one.

Family Spiritual Practice

- Show the kids where to find the Family Spiritual Practice on the Take-Home Pages (Reproducible 11F).

Supplemental Activities

Preschoolers – No Rules

Supplies: markerboard, erasable markers

Prepare Ahead: Draw several tic-tac-toe grids on the markerboard.

SAY: Most of us know how to play tic-tac-toe. Each person chooses X or O and takes turns marking a square. The goal is to get a row of X's or a row of O's. Rules for the game are: Wait for your turn and don't mark on a square someone has already marked. Let's play a game of tic-tac-toe following the rules.

• Choose two children to play, and give each child a marker.

• Choose two more children and give them each a marker.

SAY: Let's play tic-tac-toe without any rules. Go!

• You may need to prompt the children that there are no rules, so they don't have to wait their turn and they can mark over the other child's space.

• Play several times of rules and no rules, so all the children get a chance to play.

WONDER: Which way did you like to play? Was it easier to play with rules? What if there were no rules for any game we played?

Early Elementary – Rules

SAY: Let's play a game. This game has lots of rules, but I'm going to need some help remembering them all.

• Have the children sit with you in a circle on the floor.

SAY: This game involves the alphabet. I will start. When it is your turn, you will say the next letter of the alphabet, something that starts with that letter, and a new rule everyone must follow. For example, if I start with A, I might say, "A—Apple. Pat your knees." Then we will all start patting our knees. The next person might say, "B—Boy. Sing your answer." So then, we all keep patting our knees, and from then on each person is going to sing her or his answer. The rules can change at any time, so pay attention. Let's get started.

• Start with the letter A, something that begins with the letter A, and a simple rule.

• Play until each child has an opportunity to create a rule.

Older Elementary – Write the Rules

Supplies: large sheet of butcher paper or poster paper, markers

SAY: Today's Bible story outlines some important rules from God, so we can live in right and loving relationship with God and with one another. Rules help guide us, keep us safe, and keep us in healthy relationships. In this group, we are in relationship. We care for one another, respect one another, and love one another. So, we will be writing our own set of rules as a group. Let's take some time to talk about what those rules should be and write our own top ten group rules.

• Guide the children to brainstorm important rules you might have as a group.

• Write the numbers 1–10 down one side of the poster or butcher paper. If you like, tape this to the wall as you create together.

WONDER: Why was trust important in order to complete today's challenges?

Intergenerational Activity – Learning from Others

Supplies: paper, pencils, clipboards, smartphone or mobile device that records video

Prepare Ahead: Invite certain older members to be interviewed by the class. Select members whom you have seen interacting well with your class over the past quarter. You'll want to invite members who will not be shy about having their interview recorded.

• Divide the kids into groups containing a mix of older and younger kids.

SAY: We have been getting to know some older members of our church family. Today, let's interview some members.

• Invite the kids to think of some questions they'd like to ask. For example, the kids may wonder how long older members have been part of the church community. Encourage the kids to ask questions related to the faith of the elders.

• Have the kids write down their questions on a sheet of paper, using the clipboards and pencils.

• Invite the kids to use a smartphone or other mobile device to record their interviews. One kid should hold the device and record, while others ask questions.

• Be sure to have the kids thank the older member for recording an interview. Watch or listen to the interviews together as a class.

The LORD your God is with you wherever you go. (Joshua 1:9b)

A House for God – Exodus 25:1–31:18; 35:4–40:38

Prepare to Wonder

Faith Word: TRUST

The Israelites spent forty years wandering in the wilderness. They were not wandering aimlessly, though. God would speak to Moses and give him directions to relay to the Israelite people. God said to Moses, "They should make me a sanctuary so I can be present among them" (Exodus 25:8). God gave Moses specific instructions on how to build the Tabernacle and what gifts the people should bring to complete it. God also gave Moses instructions to build a special chest to carry the Ten Commandments. This special chest is also known as the ark of the covenant.

After many years of wandering, the Israelite people finally came to trust Moses and God. They eagerly brought material gifts to build the Tabernacle. They also offered their talent and skills. They brought so much that Moses asked them to stop giving!

The Israelites were constantly moving, so they needed a worship space they could carry with them. The Tabernacle was made out of cloth, more like a tent. It was important for the Israelites to have a physical reminder of God to carry with them. Many of the countries they traveled through worshipped other gods. God did not want the Israelites to forget the God that saved them.

All of the time in the wilderness, the Israelites were waiting—waiting to arrive at the land God promised them, waiting to have a real home, waiting to have a permanent place to worship God.

Spiritual Practice for Adults

Waiting often means letting go of control. What are you waiting for? Surrender your expectations to God. Carry a reminder of God with you as you wait, trusting that God will be with you through it all. Thank God for always being with you.

Come Together

Come Together

Supplies: Class Pack, Celebrate Wonder Bible Storybook, Wonder Box, green cloth, battery-operated candle, picture or small model of the Tabernacle

Prepare Ahead: Set up a Wonder Table (see p. 3) with a green cloth, battery-operated candle, and a Wonder Box (see p. 3). Display the Unit 3 Bible Verse Poster (Class Pack—pp. 9 & 16) and Faith Word Poster (Class Pack—p. 22). Place the Tabernacle inside the Wonder Box.

- Point to the Unit 3 Faith Word Poster, and invite the children to wonder about what the word *trust* means.

- Invite the kids to join you in a circle.

SAY: Last month we heard about Moses and how the Hebrew people were rescued from danger in Egypt. This month we are learning what happened next.

- Read today's story from the *Celebrate Wonder Bible Storybook.* You can allow an elementary kid to read, "A House for God" (pp. 64–65), from the storybook to the preschoolers.

- Invite the kids to share their favorite part of the story.

PRAY: Dear God, thank you for providing times for worship for us. Help us to learn how to worship you. Amen.

A House for God – Preschool

Supplies: Reproducible Kids' Book, crayons or markers

Prepare Ahead: Photocopy Reproducible 12A for each preschooler.

- Give each preschooler a copy of "A House for God" (Reproducible 12A).

SAY: God instructed the people to build a place for worship. The place was called the Tabernacle.

ASK: Where do you feel close to God?

- Share a place you feel close to God with the preschoolers.

A House for God – Younger Elementary

Supplies: Reproducible Kids' Book, crayons or colored pencils

Prepare Ahead: Photocopy Reproducible 12A for each child.

- Hand out a copy of "A House for God" (Reproducible 12A) to each child. This is the same coloring page you may have handed out to the preschoolers.

- Direct the kids to look over the page from Reproducible 12A.

SAY: In today's Bible story, God instructs the Hebrew people to make a special place to worship God. The special place was called the Tabernacle. God gave instructions to artists for building everything needed in the Tabernacle.

- Instruct the kids to color the page.

Commandment Matching – Older Elementary

Supplies: Bibles, Reproducible Kids' Book, colored pencils

Prepare Ahead: Photocopy Reproducible 12B for each child.

- Hand out a copy of "November Bible Verse" (Reproducible 12B) to each kid. You may choose to hand this sheet out to both younger- and older-elementary kids.

SAY: The Hebrew people left the land of Egypt. They started wandering in the desert. Wherever the people traveled, God was with them. Color in the letters from this month's Bible verse.

- Have the kids read the words of the Bible verse aloud as a group.

Ark of the Covenant – All Ages

Supplies: Reproducible Kids' Book; blankets, sheets, pillows, chairs, tables, other items for building a "fort"; arks made in last week's session (see p. 89)

Prepare Ahead: Make a few photocopies of Reproducible 12D. You don't need one for every kid. Instead, groups of two to three kids can share a sheet.

- Hand out copies of "The Tabernacle" (Reproducible 12D).

- Invite the kids to look over the sheets.

SAY: God instructed the Hebrew people to make a place for worship. The place God wanted the people to make was like a big tent. Let's make our own big tent!

- Invite the kids to work together to make a large tent or "pillow fort" in the classroom using tables and chairs draped with sheets and blankets. The tent should be big enough for your whole class to crawl/gather inside.

- Have the kids use blankets, pillows, and other items to "furnish" the tent.

- Invite the kids to bring the arks they may have made last week into the tent. Remind the kids about the clay tablets they may have put inside their arks.

- Invite the class to gather inside the large tent they made.

SAY: When the Tabernacle was finished, the people brought the ark of the covenant into the worship space.

- You may choose to read the Bible passage and worship inside the tent your class made this week and next week.

Wonder Time

Interactive Bible Story

Supplies: Reproducible Kids' Book

Prepare Ahead: Photocopy the Take-Home Pages from the Reproducible Kids' Book, 12F–12G (pp. 93–94).

- "A House for God" is written in short sections that are one to three sentences long. Invite several readers to take turns reading the story one section at a time.

- Read through the story.

Share a Story

Supplies: Celebrate Wonder DVD, TV, DVD player

- Invite the children to join you, sitting in a circle on the floor.
- Watch the Session 12 video (Celebrate Wonder DVD).

Wonder with Me

Supplies: Class Pack, Wonder Box, scissors, tape

Prepare Ahead: Lay out the Unit 3 Wonder Story Mat (Class Pack—pp. 11 & 14). Cut out the two remaining Unit 3 Bible story figures (Class Pack—p. 3), if not already done.

- Place the Wonder Box on the Unit 3 Wonder Story Mat.

SAY: Today's faith word is *trust.*

- Show the children the Unit 3 Faith Word Poster (Class Pack—p. 22).

SAY: In this unit, we define *trust* as believing God's love is always with you.

WONDER together:

  ❍ Why do you think God wanted the people to build the Tabernacle?

  ❍ What gifts would you offer to help build the Tabernacle?

  ❍ Can you choose which figure goes with the Bible story?

- Have a child place the tent figure on the Unit 3 Wonder Story Mat.
- Open the Wonder Box to reveal the Tabernacle.

WONDER: What do you think the Tabernacle smelled like? How big do you think it was?

Experience Wonder

The Tabernacle

Supplies: white construction paper or posterboard; red, blue, purple, copper, gold, silver crayons; aluminum foil; gold paper; red, blue, purple squares of fabric; small craft sticks; shiny chenille stems; pieces of leather; beads; glue; crayons and markers

Prepare Ahead: Lay out all the art supplies on the table.

- Have the children glue the items on the construction paper to make a tabernacle.

SAY: Our churches all look different. They might be made of brick or wood. They may have stained glass windows, or not. Some are big, and some are small. God gave Moses specific instructions on how to build the Tabernacle.

WONDER: Do you think it matters to God if our churches are different? Do you think we have items in our churches like items they might have had in the Tabernacle? What would they be?

Examine the Bible Verse

SAY: Our Unit 3 Bible verse is Joshua 1:9b. Find it in your Bibles.

ASK: Is the Book of Joshua in the Old or New Testament? *(Old)*

ASK: Where is Joshua located in the Old Testament? *(sixth book)* What is the chapter number? *(1)* What is the verse number? *(9b)*

- Gather the kids around the Unit 3 Bible Verse Poster (Class Pack—pp. 9 & 16). Read it together.

ASK: What is the reference for our verse? *(Joshua 1:9b)*

Peaceful Place

Supplies: Celebrate Wonder Bible Storybook; suggested books: "This Is the Church" by Sarah Raymond Cunningham, "Rose Guide to the Tabernacle"; building blocks; small gift boxes; glue; ribbon; stick-on gems; crayons or markers

- Assist the children, as needed, as they interact with the items provided.
- Let the children each decorate a small gift box.

- Let the children build the Tabernacle or the church using blocks.

Tip: All of the supplies/activities suggested for the Peaceful Place are optional.

Go in Peace

Spiritual Practice – Exploring Trust Through Waiting

SAY: A spiritual practice is something we do to help us connect to God. It doesn't have to be the same spiritual practice all the time, but it can be. There is no right or wrong way to do a spiritual practice. Connecting to God is the most important reason for a spiritual practice. Our church is a special place, just like the Tabernacle was for the Israelites. The church is a building, but it is also all the people who worship together.

- Guide the children through this spiritual practice.
  - ○ Say and show the children the rhyme, "This Is the Church.":
    This is the church. This is the steeple. Open the doors, and see all the people!
  - ○ Lead the children in the rhyme and motions several times.

PRAY: Repeat after me: "God, thank you for the church and all the people who worship with me. Amen."

- Bless the children before they leave. Touch each child as you say this blessing: "May you be blessed by trusting God."

- Send home a photocopy of the Family Letter (Leader Guide—p. 112) and a photocopy of the Celebration Chart (Leader Guide—p. 111) with any child who does not already have one.

Family Spiritual Practice

- Show the kids where to find the Family Spiritual Practice on the Take-Home Pages (Reproducible 12F).

Supplemental Activities

Preschoolers – Building Center

Supplies: blocks, blankets, chairs, table, large box, gold paper, tape, shiny cloth, candlesticks, biblical dress-up clothes

- Have the children use the materials to build a tabernacle.

- Have the children decorate the large box to be the ark of the covenant.

- Let the children dress up and reenact the Bible story.

SAY: Every time the Israelites would move, they had to pack up the Tabernacle and carry everything to the next campsite.

WONDER: How long do you think it took to build the Tabernacle? What would we use today to build a house for God?

Early Elementary – Building the Tabernacle

Supplies: plates, napkins, graham crackers, icing in piping bags, decorating candies, hand-washing supplies

SAY: If you were going to build a tent for God, what would it look like? Let's build tabernacles together and have a yummy snack.

- Make sure to check for food allergies, and have the children wash their hands.

- Give each child a plate and a napkin.

- Place a plate of graham crackers, a plate of decorating candies, and the icing in piping bags in the middle of the table for the children to share.

- Encourage the children to use the materials to build their own tabernacles.

- Invite children who would like to share their design with the group to do so.

- Enjoy the snack together

Older Elementary – Stained Glass Art

Supplies: Sharpie markers (variety of colors), transparency film, tin foil, card stock or cardboard, clear packing tape, ribbon or yarn, scissors

SAY: Christians have used symbols of the faith for many years. These symbols serve a purpose to remind us of who we are, who God is, and the story of God and God's people. Many times we see these symbols in Christian literature, in our church buildings, or on stained glass. Today you are going to draw one of your own or draw a heart to create stained glass art.

- The children will draw a heart (or a symbol of their choosing) onto a clear piece of transparency film using a black Sharpie marker.

- Next, they will use the Sharpie markers to color in the symbol.

- Once these are colored, give each child a piece of tin foil and a piece of card stock or cardboard that would fit in the background of their art. They will fold the tin foil around the card stock or cardboard.

- They will lay this foil-covered cardboard/card stock behind the transparency film they drew the heart/symbol on. Use clear packing tape around the edges of the pieces to help them hold together.
- If you like, add holes and a piece of ribbon to the top to hang these beautiful stained glass art creations!

Intergenerational Activity – Explore the Sanctuary

Supplies: Reproducible Kids' Book, pencils, clipboards

Prepare Ahead: Photocopy "Explore the Sanctuary" (Reproducible 12C) for each group.

- Put the kids, youth, and adults into groups. Then hand out copies of the reproducible page to the groups. Give each group a clipboard and a pencil.

SAY: God instructed the people to make a house for God. In the house of God, there were items used for worship. What do we use in worship? Let's explore the sanctuary of our church.

- Invite the groups to explore your church's sanctuary or worship space. The items listed on the reproducible page may or may not be part of your church's worship space. That's okay. Instruct the kids to check off those items they do find.

ASK: What did you find in the sanctuary *(worship space)*? Was there anything on your sheet that you couldn't find?

- Invite the groups to share what they found. Encourage the groups to discuss what the various items mean in terms of worship.

The Lord your God is with you wherever you go. (Joshua 1:9b)

Elizabeth and Zechariah – Luke 1:5-25

Prepare to Wonder

Faith Word: TRUST

This week we are wrapping up our unit on trust: believing God's love is always with you. We also celebrate the first Sunday of Advent, the Sunday of Hope. The Bible story takes place at a time King Herod ruled over Judea. Elizabeth and Zechariah really wanted children, but had made it into old age without ever having a baby.

Zechariah was a priest at the temple. One day while Zechariah was burning incense in the temple, the angel Gabriel appeared to him. As usual, Gabriel told Zechariah not to be afraid. Then he amazed Zechariah by telling him Elizabeth would be having a child, a boy, and they were to name the boy John.

Zechariah could not believe what the angel said. After all, he and Elizabeth were past the age of having children. Since Zechariah did not trust what the angel said, Gabriel told him he would lose his voice until the child was born, and he did.

Like most pregnant women, Elizabeth probably spent her pregnancy waiting and dreaming about the new baby. She was probably filled with hope for the boy who would be born.

By the time the baby was born, Zechariah trusted what the angel had said. When it came time to name and present the child at the temple, Elizabeth and Zechariah named the boy John, as God instructed them. Immediately, Zechariah's voice was restored, the time of waiting was over, and Zechariah's trust in God was strong.

Spiritual Practice for Adults

This is the first Sunday of Advent, a time of waiting for Jesus to be born. Light a candle and sit quietly. Zechariah and Elizabeth longed for a child. What longings have you hoped for? Have you waited so long, you have given up on the longings coming true? Pray that you will continue to trust God and God's timing.

Come Together

Come Together

Supplies: Class Pack, Celebrate Wonder Bible Storybook, Wonder Box, purple cloth, battery-operated candle, nametag for each child

Prepare Ahead: Set up a Wonder Table (see p. 3) with a purple cloth, battery-operated candle, and a Wonder Box (see p. 3). Display the Unit 3 Bible Verse Poster (Class Pack—pp. 9 & 16) and Faith Word Poster (Class Pack—p. 22). Place the nametags inside the Wonder Box.

- Point to the Unit 3 Faith Word Poster, and invite the children to wonder about what the word *trust* means.

- Invite the kids to join you in a circle.

SAY: We have been learning about Old Testament stories. But today we will learn something new. Today's story helps us get ready to hear about Jesus being born.

- Read today's story from the *Celebrate Wonder Bible Storybook.* You can allow an elementary kid to read, "Elizabeth and Zechariah" (pp. 190–191), from the storybook to the preschoolers.

- Invite the kids to share their favorite part of the story.

PRAY: Dear God, thank you for giving messages to people. Your messages to people help us know how much you love us. Amen.

Elizabeth and Zechariah – Preschool

Supplies: Reproducible Kids' Book, crayons or markers

Prepare Ahead: Photocopy Reproducible 13A for each preschooler.

- Give each preschooler a copy of "Elizabeth and Zechariah" (Reproducible 13A).

SAY: Zechariah was working in the temple. Suddenly, an angel appeared with a message for Zechariah. He and Elizabeth were going to have a baby! Color the picture.

Hidden Pictures – Younger Elementary

Supplies: Reproducible Kids' Book, crayons or colored pencils

Prepare Ahead: Photocopy Reproducible 13B for each child.

- Hand out a copy of "Hidden Pictures" (Reproducible 13B) to each child.

- Direct the kids to look over the page from Reproducible 13B.

ASK: What do you see on the page?

SAY: Zechariah was working in the temple, when an angel appeared with a message. But some items don't belong in the story. Can you find the hidden items?

- Instruct the kids to find the hidden items on the page. Have the kids circle the hidden items.
- Next, have them color the page.

Name Sorting – Older Elementary

Supplies: *Reproducible Kids' Book, pencils*

Prepare Ahead: *Photocopy Reproducible 13C for each child.*

- Hand out a copy of "Name Sorting" (Reproducible 13C) to each kid.

SAY: We have learned names from both the Old and New Testaments this month. Look at the list of names on the page. Then sort the names onto the correct puzzle.

- Invite the kids to use the letters in each puzzle to find a solution. The number of letters in each name can also be a clue.
- The kids may work together to solve the puzzles.

The Tabernacle and the Temple – All Ages

Supplies: *Reproducible Kids' Book, crayons or markers*

Prepare Ahead: *Photocopy Reproducible 13D for each child.*

- Hand out a copy of "The Tabernacle and the Temple" (Reproducible 13D) to each kid.

SAY: When the Hebrew people left Egypt, they began wandering in the wilderness. God instructed the people to build a house for God called the Tabernacle. Later, when the people settled in their own land, God instructed them to build a temple.

- Remind the kids about the tent your class may have made from blankets and other items last week. The Tabernacle was a portable worship space.

SAY: The temple was made many years later. It was a permanent structure for worshipping God. Today's Bible story takes place in the temple.

- Have the kids color the pictures of the Tabernacle and the temple as you discuss the two worship spaces.

ASK: Where do we worship God?

- Invite the kids to think about your church building. Mention other churches or places of worship the kids know about.

ASK: What are some other places we can worship God?

- Invite the kids to think about worshipping at home, in nature, and other places.

Wonder Time

Interactive Bible Story

Supplies: *Reproducible Kids' Book*

Prepare Ahead: *Photocopy the Take-Home Pages from the Reproducible Kids' Book, 13F–13G (pp. 95–96).*

- "Elizabeth and Zechariah" is written in short sections that are one to three sentences long. Invite several readers to take turns reading the story one section at a time.

- Read through the story.

Share a Story

Supplies: *Celebrate Wonder DVD, TV, DVD player*

- Invite the children to join you, sitting in a circle on the floor.

- Watch the Session 13 video (Celebrate Wonder DVD).

Wonder with Me

Supplies: *Class Pack, Wonder Box, scissors*

Prepare Ahead: *Lay out the Unit 3 Wonder Story Mat (Class Pack—pp. 11 & 14). Cut out the angel Bible story figure (Class Pack—p. 3), if not already done.*

- Place the Wonder Box on the Unit 3 Wonder Story Mat.

SAY: Today's faith word is *trust*.

- Show the children the Unit 3 Faith Word Poster (Class Pack—p. 22).

SAY: The definition for *trust* is believing God's love is always with you.

WONDER together:

  ❍ How do you think Zechariah felt when the angel Gabriel appeared to him?

  ❍ How did Zechariah and Elizabeth feel when they heard they would have a child?

- Have a child place the figure of the angel onto the Wonder Story Mat.
- Open the Wonder Box to reveal the nametags.

WONDER: Why do you think we have nametags in the Wonder Box?

- Help each child write his or her name on a nametag and place it on his or her clothes.

Experience Wonder

Stars and Constellations

Supplies: Reproducibles 5D and 13E, colored pencils

Prepare Ahead: Photocopy Reproducibles 5D and 13E for each kid in your class.

- Invite the kids to place both reproducible sheets in front of them on the table. Have them place the October sheet (Reproducible 5D) on the left and the November sheet (Reproducible 13E) on the right.

SAY: This fall we have been learning about stars and constellations. Look at the two sheets. The first sheet is from October. The second sheet is from November. Can you find the stars and constellations found on both of the sheets?

- Invite the kids to work together to find which stars and constellations appear on both sheets. Have the kids use a colored pencil to circle those star pictures on both sheets.

SAY: Stars move across the sky throughout the night. Each night the star pictures change just a little bit. This winter we'll get new star charts. You'll see some old star pictures and some new star pictures.

- Invite the kids to take the sheets home and look at the sky!

SAY: Looking at stars gives me a sense of awe and wonder.

Examine the Bible Verse

SAY: Our Unit 3 Bible verse is Joshua 1:9b. Find it in your Bibles.

ASK: Is the Book of Joshua in the Old or New Testament? *(Old)*

ASK: Where is Joshua located in the Old Testament? *(sixth book)* What is the chapter number? *(1)* What is the verse number? *(9b)*

- Gather the kids around the Unit 3 Bible Verse Poster (Class Pack—pp. 9 & 16). Read it together.

ASK: What is the reference for our verse? *(Joshua 1:9b)*

Peaceful Place

Supplies: Celebrate Wonder Bible Storybook, suggested book: "God Is With Us" by Amy Parker, child-friendly Nativity set, child-friendly Advent wreath, felt shapes to make angels, crayons or markers, paper

- Assist the children, as needed, as they interact with the items provided.

- Invite the children to draw a picture of the angel Gabriel and color the picture.

Tip: All of the supplies/activities suggested for the Peaceful Place are optional.

Go in Peace

Spiritual Practice – Exploring Trust Through Waiting

Supplies: Advent wreath with candles (or Class Pack—p. 23, scissors, tape)

SAY: For the next four weeks of Advent, we will do something different for the spiritual practice. We will light the Advent wreath. Lighting the Advent wreath is one way we can prepare our hearts for Jesus. The candle we light today is the candle of hope. We have hope when we trust that something will happen, even if we have to wait for it. During Advent, we hope because we trust that Jesus will be born.

SAY: As I light the first candle, say the Bible verse together, "The LORD your God is with you wherever you go."

PRAY: Repeat after me: "God, help me trust in your love and wait patiently. Amen."

- Bless the children before they leave. Touch each child as you say this blessing: "May you be blessed in the waiting."

Family Spiritual Practice

- Show the kids where to find the Family Spiritual Practice on the Take-Home Pages (Reproducible 13F).

Supplemental Activities

Preschoolers – Advent Countdown

Supplies: 27 strips of purple construction paper and 1 strip of white construction paper for each child, glue or tape, scissors

Prepare Ahead: Cut the strips and separate them for each child.

- Show the children how to loop the strips together and glue or tape to create a chain. Place the white strip at the end of the chain.

SAY: In our Bible story today, Zechariah and Elizabeth waited for their baby to be born. It can be hard to trust God when we have to wait.

SAY: Today is also the first day of Advent. Advent is a time of waiting. We are waiting for Christmas and the day Jesus was born.

- Tell the children to take the Advent chain home and, each day, take off one purple loop. When the only loop left is the white one, it will be Christmas Day.

WONDER: Is it hard to believe or trust that something you are excited about will happen? Do you trust that the celebration of Jesus' birth will happen every year?

Early Elementary – Name Bracelets

Supplies: *bowls or trays, letter beads, chenille stems*

SAY: The angel said that Zechariah and Elizabeth should name their son John. Do you know where your name came from?

- Place bowls or trays of letter beads in the center of the table.

- Give each child a chenille stem.

- Encourage the children to use the letter beads and chenille stems to create a bracelet with their names on them.

- If there are enough supplies and time, allow the children to make bracelets for friends and family as well.

Older Elementary – Musical Chairs

Supplies: *chairs in a circle, enough for all participants; music*

SAY: Waiting can also be active. Many times, our faith is called into trusting but also participating in God's mission in our world. It can seem like a conflicting thing, but it is an important part of the message of Advent. Let's play a game of musical chairs to see what I'm talking about.

- Instructions:
  - ○ Play a game of musical chairs. First, create a circle of chairs with space around them for movement. Invite a child to sit in each chair, with one person who is up and circling around the outside of the chairs. When the music plays, all participants must move. There should always be one less chair than people playing this game. Play the music and, when it stops, everyone must find a seat. Whoever is left standing is out, and a chair is also taken out. Play until there is a final person standing, the winner!

WONDER: I wonder what this game might teach us about how we wait actively as Jesus' followers.

Intergenerational Activity – Thanksgiving Board

Supplies: bulletin board and borders, banner paper, colored card stock, construction paper, stickers, crayons, colored pencils, markers, pushpins

Tip: You and your church family may have enjoyed the Thanksgiving holiday. Use this activity to help promote a spirit of thanksgiving year round.

- Invite the kids in your class to work with youth and adults to create a Thanksgiving Board for your church.

- Decorate the Thanksgiving Board using the supplies.

- Encourage the kids, youth, and adults to make notes and drawings expressing feelings of thanksgiving.

- Invite other people in your church to add to the board throughout the year. You may ask your pastor or other staff to help promote the Thanksgiving Board.

- Be creative. As the messages of thanksgiving increase over time, add pictures of your church family engaged in programs, activities, and service projects.

ASK: What are we thankful for?

- Take time to discuss the messages of thanksgiving on the board.

SAY: We have so many things to thank God for!

Celebration Chart

Place this chart on your refrigerator, kitchen table, or in an easy-to-access place. Throughout the week, have your child mark a space each time he or she completes an item on the chart. When a vertical, horizontal, or diagonal line is completed, celebrate together!

CELEBRATE

I made peace after a fight.	I tried to see someone else's view.	I showed peace.	I prayed for peace.	I was kind to a family member.
I wondered about something.	I noticed awe in nature.	I asked a hard question.	I saw God working in the world.	I learned something new.
I trusted God.	I was trustworthy today.	Free Celebration!	I shared something important with a friend or family member.	I trusted in God's love.
I prayed.	I spent time with my Bible.	I wondered about a Bible story.	I talked about a Bible story.	I learned a new Bible story.
I played with a new friend.	I went outside.	I cooked something.	I saw God in a friend.	I helped someone in my family.

Who is your family? Families come in different shapes and sizes, including those we live with, extended family, and even chosen family. In Scripture, we read about all different kinds of families who are learning and growing together. They often struggled to get along and show love to one another. Maybe this is challenging for your family too. Perhaps someone gets jealous of a sibling like Joseph's brothers, or maybe takes out their frustration on one another like the Israelites in the wilderness. This struggle can make it hard to live together and love one another as God has asked of us.

So, how do we learn to get along?

One way is learning how to deal with conflict. Conflict isn't always a bad thing because it can help us grow to be more like Jesus. But it all depends on how we respond when conflict arises! Sometimes we get so caught up in what we want to say that we forget to listen to what our family might need from us. When conflict arises, try saying to the other person, "I'm listening." Let them share why they're upset. Then, when they finish sharing, that person will tell you they're listening to you and give you the time to show that you've listened to what they need. This takes a lot of practice, so don't worry if it's hard for your family for a while. Practicing this skill will help you love your family well.

Another way we can learn to get along with our family is by using rules of boundaries. In the Book of Exodus, God gave the Israelites the Ten Commandments to help them live together well and honor God. Try making a list of rules with your family on a large piece of paper. You can write them out as statements or draw pictures to represent each one. If everyone helps make the list, everyone will feel they have a bit of ownership. Once complete, each person in your family commits that they will do their best to follow these rules as a way of showing love. Post this list in a common area of your home to remind everyone of the commitment they made.

Here are some examples of rules your family could make together:

We will give second chances.
We will tell the truth.
We will share.
We will be grateful for what we have.

What others could your family add?

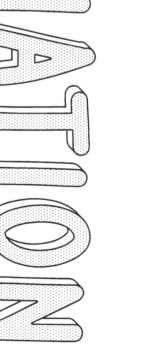

CELEBRATE WONDER

RECONCILIATION

Faith Word—Unit 1

Faith Word—Unit 2

CELEBRATE WONDER®

Faith Word—Unit 3

CELEBRATE WONDER
Using This Kit in a One-Room Ministry

Everything you need to lead faith formation with all ages in one classroom is found in this Kit.

Each week start by reviewing the session. Read the "Prepare to Wonder" section and do the spiritual practice for adults. This background information helps you navigate any questions your class may have. The spiritual practice helps prepare your heart for the coming class time.

When your class gathers, start by inviting the children into the classroom to mark their attendance on the Attendance Chart (Class Pack). Tell the children what Faith Word they will learn about that week. Let the children choose to do something from the Peaceful Place while you wait to start.

When you are ready to begin, invite all the children to join you to read the story from the *Celebrate Wonder Bible Storybook*. Then guide the preschoolers to do the coloring page, the younger-elementary kids to do their reproducible, and the older-elementary kids to do their reproducible. There is also always one activity everyone can do together. You may choose to do this instead of or in addition to the reproducible activities.

Next, your whole class will participate in an interactive retelling of the Bible story, watch the session's video from the *Celebrate Wonder DVD,* and wonder together. You will use the Wonder Story Mat (Class Pack), Faith Word Poster (Class Pack), and Wonder Box (see p. 3) during this time.

Then your class will respond to the story. There are activities to choose from: an all-ages activity, the Peaceful Place, and supplemental activities.

Finally, you will gather the group back together to participate in a spiritual practice and a blessing. You will send home the Take-Home Reproducible that has a retelling of the week's Bible story, a spiritual practice for the family to do together that week, and a pen-and-paper activity that each child can do on her or his own that week.

We have also included supplemental activities—one for preschoolers, one for early-elementary kids, one for older-elementary kids, and one for intergenerational groups. If your group leans more heavily with one of these ages, you are welcome to include one of these activities in your session.

You know your kids best. You know your volunteers best.

Some groups prefer to have more time to work alone, and some prefer to have more time to work together.

Some volunteers want to be able to choose their own activities, and some want you to have worked all of that out before they enter the room to lead the session. The most important part of ministry is connecting with one another as you grow together in God's love.

Everything you need to lead faith formation with each age group in their own space is found in this Kit.

Each week start by reviewing the session. Read the "Prepare to Wonder" section and do the spiritual practice for adults. This background information helps you navigate any questions your class may have. The spiritual practice helps prepare your heart for the coming class time. Include this page in the packet you prepare for each volunteer.

Preschool Groups

Start by inviting the children into their classrooms to mark their attendance on the Attendance Chart (Class Pack). Tell the children what Faith Word they will learn that week. Let the children choose to do something from the Peaceful Place while you wait to start.

When you are ready to begin, invite all of the children to join you to read the story from the *Celebrate Wonder Bible Storybook*. Then guide the preschoolers to do the coloring page. Next, your class will listen to an interactive retelling of the Bible story, watch the session's video from the *Celebrate Wonder DVD*, and wonder together. You will use the Wonder Story Mat (Class Pack), Faith Word Poster (Class Pack), and Wonder Box (see p. 3) during this time.

Then your class will respond to the story. There are activities to choose from: an any-ages activity, the Peaceful Place, and the supplemental activity for preschoolers. Choose one activity for everyone to do together, and then allow the children to play in the Peaceful Place.

Early Elementary Groups

Start by inviting the children into their classrooms to mark their attendance on the Attendance Chart (Class Pack). Tell the children what Faith Word they will learn that week. Let the children choose to do something from the Peaceful Place while you wait to start.

When you are ready to begin, invite all of the children to join you to read the story from the *Celebrate Wonder Bible Storybook*. Then invite the children to do the early-elementary reproducible page. There is also always one Come Together activity that you can choose to include. You may choose to do this instead of or in addition to the reproducible page.

Next, your class will read an interactive retelling of the Bible story, watch the session's video from the *Celebrate Wonder DVD,* and wonder together. You will use the Wonder Story Mat (Class Pack), Faith Word Poster (Class Pack), and Wonder Box (see p. 3) during this time.

Then your class will respond to the story. There are activities to choose from: an any-ages activity, the Peaceful Place, and the early-elementary supplemental activity. Choose one activity for everyone to do together and then allow the children to play in the Peaceful Place.

Older Elementary Groups

Start by inviting the children into their classrooms to mark their attendance on the Attendance Chart (Class Pack). Tell the children what Faith Word they will learn that week. Let the children choose to do something from the Peaceful Place while you wait to start.

When you are ready to begin, invite the children to do the older-elementary reproducible page. Do the all-ages Come Together activity in addition to the reproducible page.

Next, your class will perform the interactive retelling of the Bible story, watch the session's video from the *Celebrate Wonder DVD,* and wonder together. You will use the Wonder Story Mat (Class Pack), Faith Word Poster (Class Pack), and Wonder Box (see p. 3) during this time.

Then your class will respond to the story. There are activities to choose from: an any-ages activity, the Peaceful Place, and the older-elementary supplemental activity. Choose one activity for everyone to do together and then allow the children to play in the Peaceful Place.

Everyone will end their time together this way:

Finally, you will gather the group back together to participate in a spiritual practice and a blessing. You will send home the Take-Home Reproducible that has a retelling of the week's Bible story, something for the family to do together that week, and a pen-and-paper activity that each child can do on his or her own that week.

Start with the Large Group Time:

1. Everyone will watch the session's video from the DVD.

2. Wonder together using the unit's Wonder Story Mat and Faith Word Poster found in the Class Pack. Show the class what is in the Wonder Box and ask them what that might have to do with this week's story.

3. Send the kids to their small groups.

Small Group Time:

1. Invite the children into their classrooms to mark their attendance on the Attendance Chart (Class Pack).

2. Read the Bible story from the *Celebrate Wonder Bible Storybook* or the Bible.

3. Do the reproducible that coordinates with the age group of your small group.

4. Do the any-ages activity, the interactive retelling of the Bible story, and then allow the children to play in the Peaceful Place.

5. Gather the group back together to participate in a spiritual practice and a blessing. You will send home the Take-Home Reproducible that has a retelling of the week's Bible story, something for the family to do together that week, and a pen-and-paper activity that each child can do on her or his own that week.

If your Small Group needs more:

We have also included supplemental activities—one for preschoolers, one for early-elementary kids, and one for older-elementary kids. If your group leans more heavily with one of these ages, you are welcome to include one of these activities in your session.

CELEBRATE WONDER

Using This Kit with Large and Small Groups

The Leader Guide will have to be moved around to create an easy-to-follow plan for your volunteer teachers. The easiest way to do this is to:

1. Open the PDF of the Leader Guide.

1a. If you have Adobe Acrobat Pro, go to File>Save As>Microsoft Word>Word Document. This will turn the PDF into a Word file.

1b. If you don't have Adobe Acrobat Pro, open Microsoft Word. You will select the text from the PDF and then paste it into the Word file.

2. Arrange the activities from each session in the order that makes the most sense for your kids and volunteers.

3. Print your version of the plan and place it in each classroom.

4. Email your version of the plan to your volunteers.

Everything you need to lead faith formation with all ages, including youth and adults, in one classroom is found in this Kit.

Each week start by reviewing the session. Read the "Prepare to Wonder" section and do the spiritual practice for adults. This background information helps you navigate any questions your class may have. The spiritual practice helps prepare your heart for the coming class time.

When your class gathers, start by inviting everyone into the classroom to mark their attendance on the Attendance Chart (Class Pack). Tell each participant what Faith Word they will learn about that week. Let everyone choose to do something from the Peaceful Place while you wait to start.

When you are ready to begin, invite everyone to join you to read the story from the *Celebrate Wonder Bible Storybook*. Then guide everyone to choose one of the reproducible activities to complete. There is also always one activity that everyone can do together. You may choose to do this instead of or in addition to the reproducible activities.

Next, your whole class will participate in the interactive retelling of the Bible story, watch the session's video from the *Celebrate Wonder DVD*, and wonder together. You will use the Wonder Story Mat (Class Pack), Faith Word Poster (Class Pack), and Wonder Box (see p. 3) during this time.

Then your class will respond to the story. There are activities to choose from: an all-ages activity, an intergenerational activity found in the supplemental activities' section, and the Peaceful Place. Your group should do the intergenerational activity, then they can do any of the other activities that work well for your group.

Finally, you will gather the group back together to participate in a spiritual practice and a blessing. You will send home the Take-Home Reproducible that has a retelling of the week's Bible story, something for each family to do together that week, and a pen-and-paper activity that everyone can do on his or her own that week.

Everything you need to lead faith formation with your family at home is found in this Kit.

Each week start by reviewing the session. Read the "Prepare to Wonder" section and do the spiritual practice for adults. This background information helps you navigate any questions your kids may have. The spiritual practice helps prepare your heart for the time you will spend with your family.

When you are ready to begin, invite everyone to listen as the story is read from the *Celebrate Wonder Bible Storybook*. Then guide everyone to choose one of the reproducible activities to complete.

Next, watch the session's video from the *Celebrate Wonder DVD* and wonder together. You will use the Wonder Story Mat (Class Pack), Faith Word Poster (Class Pack), and Wonder Box (see p. 3) during this time.

Then respond to the story. There are activities to choose from: an all-ages activity, any of the supplemental activities, and the Peaceful Place. Your family can do any or all of these.

Finally, you will participate in a spiritual practice and a blessing.

Everything you need to lead faith formation virtually is found in this Kit.

Each week start by reviewing the session. Read the "Prepare to Wonder" section and do the spiritual practice for adults. This background information helps you navigate any questions your kids may have. The spiritual practice helps prepare your heart for the time you will spend together.

You can:

- Email each family the reproducible pages for the week. Encourage them to print off the pages for each person in their home, or
- Mail each family the reproducible pages for the week.

Invite each family to join you through an online video conference platform, like Zoom. Make sure to email the link the morning of the online gathering to remind your families that you will be hosting a faith-formation event.

When you are ready to begin, invite everyone to listen as the story is read from the *Celebrate Wonder Bible Storybook*. Then guide everyone to choose one of the reproducible activities to complete. You can use this time while everyone is working on their reproducible pages to catch up on joys and concerns.

Next, watch the session's video from the *Celebrate Wonder Downloadable DVD* and wonder together. You will use the Wonder Story Mat, Faith Word Poster, and Wonder Box (see p. 3) during this time.

Then respond to the story by doing the suggested art activity in the Peaceful Place and watching a YouTube video of the suggested book being read.

Finally, you lead the families in a spiritual practice and a blessing.

Zoom fatigue is real, AND our families want to stay connected in safe ways. Keep this gathering under thirty minutes, and be sure to use the time to catch up. Everyone is going through collective trauma, and they need you to be present more than they need you to teach them Bible stories.

Set up a Google Classroom or a Bitmoji Classroom using the digital assets. Your families will go through the lesson as they are able each week, instead of committing to a virtual meeting time.

Check out what Erica Kozlowski at Central United Methodist is doing in her Bitmoji Sunday School Room:

https://docs.google.com/presentation/d/1dJldspSipOK3Esorwj8Gz_
d4eit7WdfWkVwHVKewt-s/edit#slide=id.p

- Look over and plan your session before you get to your class.

- Greet the children at the door and involve them immediately in the session.

- Give a five-minute warning when it's time to move to a new activity.

- Give your children leadership roles. Preschoolers can be line leaders to help the children move to the story area. Older children can read the Bible story out loud. Be sure to ask for volunteers. If a child doesn't want to read aloud, let the child pass.

- Check for allergies before serving snacks.

- Always overplan. It's better to run out of time than to run short on a lesson.

- Review the session plan for resources you might need to gather that aren't in the church supplies.

- Gain the kids' attention.

- Ask the kids to look at you. Wait until everyone is looking. It's better for teachers to say, "Point your eyes toward me," and wait for compliance instead of saying, "Stop talking, turn around, and look at me."

- Start with small consequences. When a rule is broken, assign the smallest consequence possible and see if that gets the job done.

- Using appropriate curriculum is a classroom-management strategy.

- Assigning age-appropriate work eliminates the risk of kids not being able to do the activities.

- Rehearse transitions. Most disruptions occur between activities.

- Anticipate problems and be creative in preventing or handling them.

- Turn a problematic situation into a positive learning event.

- Find things to appreciate. Start class by looking for things to delight in.

- Create an inclusive environment.

- Be clear up front about expectations and intentions.

- Use inclusive language.

- Ask for clarification if you're unclear about a kid's question.

- Treat all of your kids with respect and consideration.

- Develop an awareness of barriers to learning (cultural, social, experiential).

- Provide sufficient time and space for kids to gather their thoughts and contribute to discussions.

- Use hand signals and other nonverbal communication.

- Sometimes the behavior of a single child can become so disruptive that you can't teach the session. Get help! If certain children are repeatedly disruptive, add more adults to your group, or ask parents and caregivers for helpful ways to care for and engage their child.

CELEBRATE WONDER. Registration Page

Child's Name _____

Parent Name(s) _____

Address _____

_____

Phone _____

Child's Birthday _____ Age _____

Child's Brothers and Sisters:

Name _____ Age _____

Name _____ Age _____

Name _____ Age _____

Grandparents or other adults your child sees often and is close to:

_____

_____

Allergies or situations the teacher should know about:

_____

_____

_____

_____

Parent will be at:

_____

_____

_____

Introducing...

Cokesbury

Kids
CLUB

Sign up for the FREE Cokesbury Kids Club today!

Benefits include:

- FREE monthly e-book!
- First look at new VBS themes, curriculum, and products!
- Special offers and discounts!
- And much more!

Find out more at the ALL-NEW CokesburyKids.com!